BARRIS KUSTOM INDUSTRIES

SURVIVOR

THE UNRESTORED COLLECTOR CAR

KRIS PALMER

PARKER
HOUSE

Parker House Publishing Inc.
1826 Tower Drive,
Stillwater, Minnesota 55082, USA
www.parkerhousepublishing.com

ISBN-13: 978-0-9817270-1-1

Book design Diana Boger
Cover design Amy Van Ert-Anderson
Editor Kristal Leebrick

Manufactured in China through World Print Ltd.

10 9 8 7 6 5 4 3 2 1

For Karl and Marilyn Palmer,
who hoped for a doctor but accepted a writer.

Contents

PART 1: THOUGHTS AND TIPS ON UNRESTORED CARS

PART 2: SURVIVOR TALES

Foreword by Tom Cotter

ABOUT TWENTY YEARS AGO, my wife, Pat, and I drove our red 1965 Porsche to a 356 Registry convention in the North Carolina mountains. The weather and roads were ideal for sports car driving, and there were perhaps one hundred of the finest-looking early Porsches of every type on display: coupes, convertibles, and Speedsters. Of all those cars, I remember one in particular, a rather raunchy and unrestored Speedster, getting much more than its share of attention.

This Speedster was ugly. The owner told me it was once silver, but the most recent paint job was at least twenty years old. Since then, it had oxidized terribly and more resembled a three-dimensional "moonscape" than a slick silver finish. The color (somewhere between dark gray and black) was covered with automotive acne.

Yet the car was intriguing and a hit with the crowd. "How long have you had it?" "When are you going to restore it?" "Is it for sale?" The owner calmly told whoever asked that he had owned the car for at least twenty-five years, he was not going to restore it and it wasn't for sale.

He had fought off the urge. Click! A light bulb turned on in my head.

It's all too easy to restore a car, or let's say it's easy to *start* a restoration. Have you ever noticed when you drag a new relic home and you're so eager to get started that the car almost comes apart by itself? First you dig for spare change from under the seats and carpets, then look in door pockets and the glove box for old matchbooks, can openers, and condoms. One thing leads to another, and by sunset you and your greasy friends are sprawled across the driveway among tools, parts, and filth. Just as you're ready to yank the engine from under the hood, your wife hollers from the kitchen that dinner is ready.

It will be at least five years and untold dollars before that car is put back together, if ever. My motto is that it's "fun" and "free" when you're twisting the bolts counter-clockwise, but it gets really expensive and time consuming when you start twisting those bolts in the other way. When restoration is completed, what you have is a sort-of "replica" of the original car.

I belong to a "secret society" of owners of original Cobras, and our mission is to keep our cars original at all costs. That means we don't restore them. You may ask, "If it's an original Cobra, why shouldn't it be restored?" The issue is that original cars were bolted together in the early 1960s at the Shelby American shops in Los Angeles by employees of Carroll Shelby. Many times the non-maintenance-related components that were put in place and tightened down by original Cobra techni-cians are still in place. But once those parts are taken off and replaced with new components (door locks, windshield, wire wheels, body panels), it becomes less original and somewhat of a replica because most new parts are sourced from the same suppliers as the replica companies use. Our group of Cobra owners will go to extremes to rebuild and re-machine parts whenever possible instead of installing a replacement. At a Cobra show, it's often the "ratty" example in the lineup that is the real one among the legions of replicas and Shelby continuation cars.

One such car is my friend Jim's 289 Cobra. Jim bought the car several decades ago when the Cobras were simply powerful sports cars and not the legendary collector cars they have become. Jim's British Racing Green Cobra is dripping with patina with its tattered paint and well-worn interior, and that's just the way he likes it. When the aluminum body gets scratched, Jim simply touches up the paint with a spray can of Rustoleum purchased from his local True Value hard-ware store. Jim enjoys the original Shelby and drives the wheels off the well-worn car throughout Southern California. With tongue in cheek, he places a sign on the windshield when he parks it at cruise-in events that reads, "Cobra Kit Car Club, Please Do Not Touch."

It's been said that Americans are too obsessed with newness and cleanliness. Where Europeans love the weathered look and character of maintained original furniture, houses, and cars, on this side of the pond we are always trying to make our flea market–found tables, chairs, and yes, cars, appear brand new. But who among us would choose to wear a stiff new pair of blue jeans rather than a pair with several years under their belt? Who wouldn't prefer to wear a twenty-year-old leather bomber jacket over a stiff new version?

An unrestored car has patina and character that a freshly minted restoration can't touch. To put it in human terms, it's the same as a weathered and wrinkled elderly man or woman who has wonderful stories to tell of a well-lived life, as opposed to a "cosmetically enhanced" person who poses and looks pretty but hasn't much personality. Restored "trailer queen" cars that have never experienced stone dings or even a squished bug on their paint are about as interesting.

Thankfully the trend of preservation seems to be catching on. Renowned collectors who are not strangers to the Amelia Island and Pebble Beach Concours events are finding it extremely gratifying to discover and maintain classic cars in their as-found condition. Roger Morrison of Kansas owns the 1929 Rolls-Royce that Hollywood diva Marlene Dietrich used when she was in Los Angeles. The car remains in the half-restored condition in which it was discovered several years ago. Morrison's Rolls was one of the stars of a six-month-long barn-find exhibit held at New York's Saratoga Auto Museum in 2007. Another highlight of the show was Jim Taylor's fabulous 1936 Horch, a huge and elegant car that rivals the grandest pre-World War II Mercedes-Benzes. Interestingly, both these cars are worth more than $1 million whether left in their as-found condition or restored.

A car can always be restored, but it is only original once.

I own a 1938 Ford Woody Wagon—not Ford's best looking model, but I love it just the same. It has never been restored, although somewhere during its seventy-year life it was painted and the seats were reupholstered. Of all the restored old Fords I've had the opportunity to drive, this woody is my favorite. Like that old pair of jeans, it's a little bit tarnished and worn around the edges, but it was put together in 1938 by Ford mechanics in Dearborn, Michigan, not some restoration shop in Anywhere, USA.

I'm too young to have purchased a new 1938 Ford, but by touching the steering wheel, shifter, and door handles when I drive this woody, I feel like I'm shaking hands with Henry Ford himself.

Tom Cotter
Author
The Cobra in the Barn and *The Hemi in the Barn*
[MBI Publishing Company 2005 and 2007 respectively]

Acknowledgments

MANY PEOPLE STEP FORWARD with information, stories, cars, entre, skills, and references when you go to write a book. The following kind, knowledgeable, and skillful individuals helped me put this one in your hands. I thank all of them for their generosity: Tom Cotter, Henry Pearman, Tom Porter, Greg Nelsen, Ed Godshalk, Stan Reeg, James Price, Mark Haines, Gene Hetland, James Maxwell, Bob Youngdahl, Red Leonard, Tom Witta, James Mann, Tim Parker, Jerry Lee, Chris Leydon, Daryl and Nate Kirt, Bo Vescio, Phyllis McClintock, Kim Ray, Joji Barris, Thomas Grubba, Genevieve, Arthur, and Maggie Shiffrar, Kandace Hawkinson, and Jeanne and Dana Breska.

Introduction

AT MOSTLY REGULAR INTERVALS throughout the warmer months, a handful of gearheads gather at a homey coffee shop in Saint Paul, Minnesota, called Swede Hollow. There, amid fact and folklore, Tim Parker and I struck up a conversation about unrestored cars, a subset of the classic car realm that we both enjoy. Long with the world's largest car-book publisher, MBI Publishing Company (formerly Motorbooks International), Tim is off on his own now publishing titles on his favorite topics.

Amped up on coffee and scones, we hashed out an idea for the book in hand. All older cars are getting rarer and those that survive the decades unrestored are an exciting and endangered species of land craft. Writing about them, ferreting out good examples and stories, sounded like great fun.

Years in a classroom, and then at a desk trying to pay them off, yield methods for hunting down and understanding most any concept. In ten years of automotive writing, I'd come across some complicated topics—never fear one so familiar as unrestored cars. A book on that subject could be tackled the same way as one on anything else, from headlights to Carroll Shelby to the Nürburgring. Or so it seemed.

Yet casting a net into the great information sea and reeling it back yielded . . . not much. There are plenty of stories and photos of unrestored cars and debates on whether particular cars, or cars generally, are better off restored or with all years showing. But definitive work—deep and thoughtful analyses of what a survivor or preserved car is and wherefrom the enthusiasm derives—was not so easy to spot in incomprehension's murky waters.

The problem with the headlight/Shelby/'Ring approach as a model for this subject is that we know what a headlight is. We know who Mr. Shelby is. We know the Nürburgring is a famous racetrack steeped in history and documentation. You can define these concepts unambiguously, hunt down their pasts, pitfalls, and pinnacles and try to present them in a fresh way.

The survivor idea is far more elusive, or maybe not nearly elusive enough. A simple description, with all of simplicity's complications, is that a survivor is an unrestored car, a car whose owners didn't change it. *Cool. Who doesn't like those?*

But beware of topics that seem basic fare. This is a concept expressed in the negative: a car that has not been changed; a vehicle that has not been restored. It's a passive concept, defined by inaction. That fact turns five-W analysis (who, what, when, where, why) on its head.

Who was the first person not to restore a car?

When did the idea of not changing anything first arise?

Provide a thorough analysis of what it means to do nothing to your automobile.

How would you advise others on leaving their cars just as they are?

What are some of the mistakes people make when undertaking inaction?

"Bartender, 'nother round of no drinks please...."

Survivors do exist. They're wonderful historical snapshots brimming with build and use history. Many have interesting stories and personalities attached. That they're difficult to define with precision is not a weakness; it's a testament to their individuality. Survivors are unique and it is that characteristic that makes them so appealing.

You can go out today and find two 1964 Pontiac GTOs, or two 1955 Ford Thunderbirds, take them to the same shop, and ask that they be restored identically. Apart from some stamped numbers, that objective is achievable. Heck, you could grind off the numbers. But the two cars before they are restored are not identical. They vary in hundreds of ways, from the obvious—a scratch or chip here, a rip there—to the very subtle. One has faded just a tiny bit more than the other. One was driven by a smoker, such that the finish on the lighter was partially polished off by the owner's fingertips; the other was used in *American Graffiti,* and the scratch made by George Lucas's clipboard as he traded a word with Suzanne Somers is still there. It's the difference each survivor has from all other cars that is the essence of the concept, and the very thing that makes confining them to a rigid list of characteristics virtually impossible.

If the survivor concept is like a pool of oil, clear but slippery, it envelopes ideas and passions well known within and beyond the automotive world. This book explores the survivor's place, pleasures, and challenges and hopefully lends some insights to those who own or contemplate buying an unrestored car. These are not the last words on a well trodden subject but early thoughts on a class of vehicles likely to grow in excitement and value for many years to come.

Part 1 looks at originality, restoration and preservation issues with an eye toward making decisions that best serve car and owner.

Part 2 tells the stories of unrestored cars of varying age, rarity, and value, as well as their owners' histories with the automobiles they cherish. We hope you enjoy them.

Thanks for making *Survivor: The Unrestored Classic Car* part of your automotive library.

—Kris Palmer, 2008

Part 1

Thoughts and Tips
on Unrestored Cars

JAMES MANN

This 1920s Rolls-Royce
40/50 bears a lovely
patina. Some eyes
search for exactly this
look; others view this car
and imagine it spotless
and gleaming following a
concours restoration.

CHAPTER 1

Great Restoration Project
—but Wait!

FOR EVERY AUTO OPTIMIST traipsing the landscape on a mission for cars, provocative vehicles wait to be found. Some are as close as the classifieds. Others lie silent under tarps and in barns, on patios, and in paddocks, alleys, and yards. A few have been pampered in homes, warehouses, garages, and hangars.

The cars we pursue in thought and action are whole—and dismembered. Many exist in an altered state, a product of their manufacturer's design supplemented by owners' additions, subtractions, modifications, and wear.

Most are known, yet there are enticing cars lost to the collector world, at least for now. Some of our quarry start and drive; others are pure potential, a mere projection of what they could be with the right attention and care.

Wherever the machines that make our dreams real, none has escaped Time's corruptive hand. As hard as we strive to mine the elements and shape them to our will, nature's forces work just as hard to break them down and return them to the earth. How broad Time's influence, and how destructive, turns on many things. We won't know the full story of a vehicle's condition until it is ours, before our eyes and lights, on our lifts.

Yet bagging automotive game—the fantasy that most preoc-cupies us—is just the beginning. What happens to a piece of automotive history under our care is up to us. We can preserve each mark our find has acquired over its lifetime, each clue as to how and where and when its drivers went motoring, or we can obliterate them all. Every maintenance and repair decision we

Gentle wear on this E-Type coupe's leather and carpets have perfect presentation for a driver. You can use the car and not grimace when some dirt or rainwater comes in on your shoes.

This rare Ford Sedan Delivery has been immaculately restored and is beautiful from all angles. Removing evidence of age does not render a car undesirable; it simply creates a different sort of appeal from one that looks old in presentation as well as design.

The American public never got to behold Chrysler's innovative Norseman. A freak accident sent it to the ocean floor, along with the equally impressive *Andrea Doria* luxury liner.

make either keeps a vehicle close to its initial form or pushes it further away.

In what condition will your next automobile come to you?

What will it become in your hands?

If the basic survivor question seems easy—do you keep a car original or restore it?—in the real world, the answer is more complex. This is true even for famous cars and singular examples.

Consider a futuristic show car aboard a state-of-the-art ocean liner. Chrysler designed the Norseman to showcase its most innovative design features. The company hired Italy's Ghia design firm to craft the car, which it did in extraordinary fashion. What better way for it to come to the United States than aboard the *Andrea Doria*, the most fashionable passenger vessel of the day? No one aboard the *Doria*, headed toward New York harbor—or the Swedish ship, *Stockholm*, departing it—could envision either ship going down . . . until the two collided.

Seizing the Norseman today would require sailing 100 miles off the Nantucket coast, diving some 240 feet into frigid salt water, entering the debris-strewn catacombs of the slumbering *Andrea Doria*, locating the car, and then extracting it through wreckage, fishing nets, and sharks. After all that, the recovered treasure would not be the Norseman as it sunk in 1956.

A famous Porsche of the same period also took a call from Bad Luck. James Dean's silver 550 Spyder was well known to his

James Dean's wrecked Porsche: What do you do when the most significant part of a car's history is its destruction? Finding and restoring Dean's Porsche would leave you with one like this—an exciting and alluring car, but one nobody would realize was the genuine Dean article.

film fans and on the local racing scene. Heading toward a quiet intersection at dusk, however, the car was nearly invisible. Like the *Andrea Doria*, the Porsche met another vehicle it could not avoid. The crash killed Dean, injured his mechanic-passenger, and crumpled the famous 550. Safe-driving advocates put the wrecked car on tour to demonstrate driving's hazards, but it disappeared. Museums, fans, and the curious of all stripes have been looking for it ever since.

Another Ghia show car, the Lincoln Futura, was transformed by a third force: customization. Since the early 1960s, it has lived in the public mind as the Batmobile, winged steed of Adam West and Burt Ward. Auto artist George Barris, who had painted "Little Bastard" on the back of Dean's Porsche, bought the Futura after its popular car-show career and an appearance in the 1959 film *It Started with a Kiss*. He redesigned and re-crafted it into Batman and Robin's ride in under three weeks.

Three famous automobiles known by millions. None exists today as it was originally built. If a car is at its best when new, or returned to new, then each of these vehicles cries out for a rescuer. The collector with the bucks and the guts should haul up the Norseman and spare no sum making it just as Ghia

Topping the Futura for all-out cool is a challenge few designers could meet . . .

. . . yet George Barris succeeded in making it even more popular and iconic by transforming it into the Batmobile. Do we recommend that anyone else cut up show cars with the same goal? No!

assembled it. The same path is best for the Dean car, if it still exists—locate, acquire, cut, straighten, repair, and replace until it is indistinguishable from the day the cool blond actor first picked up the keys. And the Futura? Pull off the bat bits, rebuild the show car.

Is it that easy? Despite decay, damage, and a later owner's modifications, none of these cars has a preferred fate all admirers could agree on. As alluring as the Norseman was, it's treasure trove now, as much a part of the *Andrea Doria*'s history as Chrysler's. Dean's Porsche was rare, but erasing the damage that killed a cinema icon—would it be right? And the Batmobile, gaped at and drawn and dreamt of and played with in

Corgi-toy form by generations of fans, should it be torn apart? Only devoted Futura-istas would say yes.

The dilemma of how to proceed with a collector car doesn't get much easier when it isn't a famous, one-of-a-kind vehicle. Restoration decisions have as many options and outcomes as there are potential buyers. Even the survivor concept isn't as simple as leaving the car alone. Many variables come into play.

Restoration—the Highest Compliment?

Who among us does not have an inoperable watch or bicycle or appliance tucked away for another day? It's a useful possession, we need or want it in our daily lives, so we'll repair or replace it—a natural, logical response. When an object that was appealing to look at becomes worn or dirty or damaged, our impulse is to renew it, to return it to its early, more pleasing state.

There's more than pragmatism at work in such decisions. The words associated with disorder and decay have a negative connotation: broken, frayed, rotted, bent, shabby, torn, faded, chipped, cracked, rusty, dull. We don't want our possessions branded substandard.

Descriptions conveying order and freshness and functionality, by contrast, are positive: clean, polished, gleaming, flawless, pristine, shining, immaculate, vibrant, like new, perfect. These terms sound flattering and refined, superior to the prior list in value and character.

This unrestored Camaro is a driver on the East Coast. When the car is younger and more common, do we see patina differently?

With such perceptions dominating our world view, removing flaws from a cherished possession like a collector car can seem not just acceptable but compulsory, the natural course for a car showing wear. For decades, restoration has been the preferred treatment for collector cars marked by their years.

The age-weary car was often sold but seldom admired "as is"; it was viewed instead as a "prime restoration candidate." Against this backdrop, the couple complacently driving a rusting Duesenberg were unworthy custodians of a piece of treasured automotive history. Someone running a faded, dinged-up vintage Ferrari lacked respect for the car's breeding, or so conventional views might have held.

These perspectives are not unique to the automobile. Fear of wear and damage, and a collective ambition to arrest them, predate the motor car by thousands of years. They are driving forces in the fields of art and archaeology. What we appreciate, admire, love to view, contemplate, or possess, we also wish to preserve—to sustain all of those benefits for ourselves and to pass them on to others. Without these motivations, many of civilization's cultural treasures would eventually decompose beyond recognition.

Among the seven ancient wonders of the world was the Colossus at Rhodes, a statue standing more than 100 feet tall by that island's harbor. Even after an earthquake felled the massive figure, people traveled great distances to see it tumbled and broken. Although impressive on the ground (Roman scholar Pliny the Elder said few people could get their arms around its thumb) talk focused on rebuilding it. Egypt's ruler even offered to fund the effort, but an oracle warned against it so the island declined. Discussions of restoring it to its former glory continued for the nearly 900 years that the massive pieces lay by the sea, until finally they were carted off.

Egyptian and Mayan pyramids, among the world's most recognizable structures, have also seen restoration efforts over the ages as wars, plunderers, weather, and tourism have wrought their wear and wreckage. Many are the subject of seemingly endless restoration discussion and debate. These monuments represent high points in human ingenuity, worth saving as historical records and for their power to inform and inspire future generations.

How best to restore or preserve something (separate from whether to do so) is a question we look to science to help us answer. Scientific advances bring new preservation methods and theories that often question what came before. Even objects sheltered in private homes and museums do not escape harm from smoke, light, humidity, water, vibration, and mishandling. The older the work, the more likely it has gotten in harm's way and that some well meaning person has tried to undo the damage.

In the fine art world, conservators wrestle daily with the forces of entropy that seek to dismantle what careful hands create. Restoration efforts can compound the damage as easily as reduce it. Solvents used to remove grime can take paint along with it. New paint blended into old paintings has not always aged the same way as the original materials, sometimes leaving discolored regions as alarming and disruptive as the initial problem.

Sustaining beautiful and important works is a calling in archaeology, architecture, art, and other fields. We could argue whether our obligations to future generations include preserving the Yugo. Cars as a whole offer less ground for debate. The automobile has captured our hearts and minds in races, shows, paintings, books, sculpture, film, television, posters, photographs, t-shirts, models, toys, ads . . . as a gift, as an escape, as evocation of freedom, beauty, and power, or efficiency or luxury or technological advancement. Flat-out or standing still, a desirable car can speak to the soul as clearly as any other work of art.

And like the millennia of art that came before it, cars face the same hurdles when we try to stop and reverse decay. Desirable cars are worth preserving, but how?

ENTROPY'S RESTLESS HANDS

In June 1957, the city of Tulsa, Oklahoma, buried a new Plymouth Belvedere Sport Coupe in its courthouse lawn. With its broad open grille, dual headlights, and high fins, the car had style, but not too much style. Chrysler's best-selling, least-expensive division, Plymouth, was a fine symbol for middle class values and, in city leaders' minds, an ideal gift to Tulsa's future. Preparing their generous bequest for its long slumber, city leaders no doubt pictured their descendants' faces as they disinterred the same gleaming embodiment of 1950s design.

When the Tulsa Plymouth was removed from the ground, the large crowd in attendance did have expressive faces, though not the delighted ones their predecessors imagined. The decayed specimen that emerged from the ground looked like it had been buried for several centuries, not half of one. Its moist tomb was more time accelerator than time capsule. After fifty years beneath the sea, the Chrysler Norseman probably looks little worse than its Tulsa cousin.

More than faded paint is at issue with this Studebaker; rust is starting to take hold. Stopping disintegration is a different question from preserving more passive imperfections.

As Neil Young so nicely put it, rust never sleeps—nor do any of the forces of decay. They work to break down modern goods with age-old fervor. The raw materials used to build a car are the same resources fashioned into other works. Artists and artisans have employed some of these materials for hundreds, even thousands, of years.

Whether the end result is a painting, statue, vase, multimedia installation, or automobile, the component parts are vulnerable to the same threats to their structural and aesthetic integrity. Water, sunlight, smoke, fire, mold, airborne contaminants, oxidation, rodents, insects, and temperature and humidity swings and extremes can wreak havoc on paint, sheet metal, leather, textiles, tires, weather stripping, dashboard, headliner, belts, water passages, fluids, lubricants, bearings, seals, and every other unprotected surface or component.

Paintwork loses its luster; it begins to fade. Encounters with car, truck, and garage doors, bicycles, footballs, basketballs,

The professional paint job on this Muntz Jet will be better and longer lasting than what the factory applied.

falling rakes, shovels, and brooms, the keys in our hands, pants rivets, belt buckles, watches, bracelets, rings, dropped wrenches, screwdrivers, and bolts leave their dings, scratches, and dents. Stones and gravel chip the finish; chemicals, soft drinks, and bird-droppings leave spots. Prolonged polishing wears off the paint. Moisture—with its accomplices, mud, snow, ice, and salt—savages exposed metal into open rusty sores.

A cloth interior doesn't age like leather.

Every day that passes sustains existing destructive forces and creates opportunity for new ones. It takes work to stop them. Letting them march on can make us feel guilty and push us toward corrective measures—like restoration.

A fresh coat of paint has a deep liquid shine you could almost dive into, to emerge in some auto nirvana where car luminaries argue and explain, draft and design, build and race. There is honor in a quality finish, and great skill behind it. An

TOM WITTA

Though it would cost a fortune, a quality restoration shop could turn parts cars like these . . .

unbroken transition from fender to door to quarter panel belies Olympic-scale efforts. It requires arduous, uncompromising surface preparation and an artist's eye. Perfection that traces an automobile's shifting contours is as elusive as a masterpiece on canvas.

Knowing what faultless paint can be, we need a sea-change in perspective to accept a finish decades on, when it is scraped, faded, and dull.

The interior has no less impact on our estimation and appreciation. Here is where our time is spent whenever the vehicle is not at rest. Complete vibrant carpets, polished wood, unfaded and uncracked leather, vinyl, plastic, and Bakelite impress and reassure us. An interior in excellent condition implies that the car's mechanicals are equally fit and we will reach our destination without pushing, towing, or thumbing a ride.

How do we find the same good feelings looking at ragged floors, a baked and shriveled dashboard, torn seats, and a pitted windshield? Where do we find comfort in lack of comfort?

Time's ravages go beyond looks. As cars age, we rely on them less. They get covered up, pushed aside. Without regular use,

routine maintenance falls off. Batteries die, belts and hoses grow brittle and crack, wiper blades harden and split, as do rubber seals on windows, doors, and trunks. What once transported or pumped or fended off water no longer does. In an age that celebrates action and achievement, can there be praise for parts past their prime?

No makeup artist or doctor can make a fifty-year-old identical to her twenty-year-old self, but a restoration shop can remove virtually every trace of wear, damage, and decay from an automobile. They can take your careworn antique, classic, or contemporary car and make it "better than new." How can we refuse such an offer?

. . . into superb collectibles like these. No similar process allows grandparents to emerge from a "shop" indistinguishable in age from their children's children.

Cars of little value
don't stir arguments
over whether or not
to restore them—
except perhaps
among spouses. This
XK120 is a different
story and would draw
eyes at any show.

CHAPTER 2

When Imperfect Is Perfect

TELEVISION'S INFLUENCE IS WANING in the Internet age, but it remains a powerful medium for disseminating ideas, even from unexpected sources. The *Antiques Roadshow* began in Britain in the late 1970s and crossed the Atlantic to appear on the American Public Broadcasting Service (PBS) in the 1990s.

Popular hunger for a program about old stuff exceeded its producers' most optimistic projections. The show won an international audience and prompted viewers to poke around their own garages and attics for potential treasures. Frequently, the show's appraisers called out originality as a key value indicator. Unrestored pieces, with the original finish and hardware, enjoyed more praise and a higher estimate. Works by well known artists and crafters that had been stripped and redone were often marked down for that reason.

As the program continued and its audience grew, a broad cross-section of the public took home the notion that restoration hurts value. So strong was this incidental message that the furniture restoration industry felt its impact. The editor of the magazine *Professional Refinishing* wrote the American show's executive producer to describe the influence it was having in his field. The producer's response explained that, while the show's appraisers enjoyed finding rare pieces in good condition, that was not the shape much old furniture was in; objects with excessive wear or damage typically did benefit from restoration. Even if the public had over-applied the value of unrestored condition, the show gave people pause in reaching for the paint stripper and polyurethane.

21

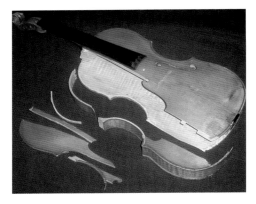

This two-century-old violin attributed to Gennaro Fabricatore of Napoli was shattered in a car accident. Repairing it required substantial work.

The goal with the finished instrument was not to make it look as though it had been beautifully repaired, but to make it look like no repair was ever undertaken or needed. This is the completed violin; it could easily pass for a pre-accident shot.

The *Antiques Roadshow* popularized the idea of leaving time's indicia alone. Older items are perceived as better made, rarer, more nostalgic and collectible than new products. Original goods are valued more highly than reproductions. If the genuine article is more desirable, why spend time and money removing the very characteristics, like patina, that distinguish it from a modern knockoff? Patina helps prove age, the aspect of a vintage or classic object that inspired our admiration in the first place. (True, patina can be mimicked, but experience will more likely encourage us to judge the pristine and polished item as new than to assume the yellowed and gently worn one has been artificially aged.)

Naturally, respect for age and originality predates the *Antiques Roadshow*, which merely brought together experts applying views from many fields developed before the show tapped them. Patrick Milan is a Minneapolis-based artisan who repairs stringed instruments. When a damaged violin—for example, one splintered in a car accident—comes into his shop, his first step in addressing it is to study the original wood and varnish and determine the intent of the instrument's maker. "We want to save as much of the original piece as possible," he says. "Even when wood or finish must be replaced, we strive to take away as little as possible, and put it back in such a way that it is indistinguishable from the original."

Gun collectors likewise value pieces that have not had their history blasted or stripped away. Bluing, the process giving unpainted gun metal its characteristic look, has been done different ways at different times and places. This finish's condition has a great deal to do with a collector gun's value. Extensive refinishing will harm the value of a rare or historically significant firearm (even if it enhances a common gun that's too rough).

Coin collectors are equally familiar with original appearances and the perils of removing them. Those numismatists who rubbed off tarnish with a pencil eraser learned too late that they had likewise scrubbed value from their collection.

All of these objects—guns, coins, furniture, instruments, and automobiles—help define the look and feel of the period during which they were made and used in daily life. Remove time's marks and the object loses its most convincing connection with the past it represents. It becomes a modern interpretation of an old item indistinguishable from a high-quality reproduction finished a week, rather than decades or centuries, ago.

As the popular saying goes, "It's only original once." When you remove the original finish and replace original parts, you sever and destroy some of the connections linking the object's present with its past. Remove all signs of age and wear and onlookers may wonder how much, if any, of the vehicle hails from the year of its purported manufacture.

Unrestored, Preserved, Original

Cars are a hobby filled with passion—and jargon. Like other hobbies, it has its own terms and slang, words other niches don't understand, or use in a different way. Even among gearheads and motor*istes* there are some divergent approaches. The survivor concept has fuzzy boundaries, as proven by the many ways sellers, buyers, and owners use it. Fortunately, the related notions of unrestored, preserved, and original cars offer some compass points. Together, they describe important principles for the future of collector cars.

In shorthand terms, a survivor is an unrestored car. Part of "survivor's" boundary blur, however, comes from "unrestored" having some definitional play of its own. Does it

The rows of shiny slugs in a hardware store are sterile and lifeless compared to a set of keys with patina.

mean "untouched" or only "not comprehensively restored." The latter includes a body-off-frame restoration, where body and chassis are separated to attack rust and remove paint above and below, and a rotisserie restoration, in which the body tub is suspended on rotating pivots so that every fault can be seen and removed. If a car has had something less than this—a quick freshen-up of the engine, some new carpets and floor mats, and a coat of paint—has it been restored? Not to a prestigious restoration house it hasn't, but calling that car "unrestored" might raise a few eyebrows at an auction.

"Preserved" gets us a little closer. That which is preserved is predominantly unchanged. "Perfectly preserved" connotes an object frozen in time, one that looks today as it did when last seen or used. Still, what are the parameters that rule a car in, or out of, this definition? Preserved *in what way*? If the whole car is there, but it's rusting and the seats are ripped with the stuffing hanging out and the gauges are cracked and the top is in shreds and the carpets are ragged, is it preserved? In the sense that you can see and touch it and identify the car and all of its parts, yes, it's preserved. It has not disappeared, been dismantled, or destroyed. But if "preserved" is a state of survival in which collectors should consider leaving the vehicle for its historic value, this one pushes limits as to

This MG has a lot of original parts but had been repainted once and that finish had faded. A few small rust spots were taking hold.

The car now wears a new coat of paint in the factory color to protect the sheet metal from further deterioration. Is this car preserved? Not quite. Restored? A little. It lies in the gray area between.

the number of faults many enthusiasts would accept over the long haul. "Worn but presentable" condition would appease more owners.

Finally, there's "original," another term that sits there looking all self-explanatory then goes coy on you as soon as you ring up for a chat. "Original owner" is a nice, straightforward term the hobby is in agreement upon. We could create ambiguity by suggesting that a dealership owns the car first, or the manufacturer, but no one understands it that way. The original owner is the one who bought the car new from a dealership or, in more limited cases, directly from the factory.

"Original" as applied to the car takes us back to familiar ambiguous territory. Everyone who reads car ads has seen listings for vehicles characterized as both "all original" and "totally restored." Foremost Insurance (part of Farmers Insurance Group), for example, includes "original restored condition" in its description of "collectible automobile." Before *Antiques Roadshow* went global and unrestored cars started attracting attention at big-time car venues, juxtaposing these statements didn't seem strange. Now, to at least a few people in the hobby, it does. What such a phrase is apparently conveying is that all the major body, interior, and mechanical components are the ones that came on the car when new. Yet if it's been totally restored, many things applied by the factory have disappeared. The original paint has been removed or covered up. Totally restored cars have perfect paint; unrestored ones don't. A lot of restorations also involve scrapping old carpets, upholstery, dash pads, headliners, trunk lining, and glass and replating bumpers and trim.

How can a "totally restored" 1965 Mustang be "all original" when so much of the factory's work has been undone? The answer involves perspective and our collective willingness to exclude some things from the originality inquiry. "Perishables," like brake pads, windshield wipers, and tires, are items that must be replaced to ensure proper functionality and safety in a car that sees ongoing use. Asking auctioneers of "all-original" cars to drop the description, or footnote it, when the brake pads have been replaced goes too far. For those extremely rare cars that still have such factory-fitted components, owners and sellers can add them to their "all-original" qualifications, pushing them beyond expectations.

Cars bearing their original perishable or "maintenance" items, along with everything else, would lie at the strictest end of the originality scale. At the other end are vehicles with original engines, transmissions, and bodies. The laxest use of "numbers-matching car" means only that the engine in it is the one the factory fitted in that particular car. Chrysler numbered many components in its muscle cars, allowing collectors to establish originality more thoroughly. "All numbers matching" promises a longer list than body and engine alone.

Increased emphasis on cars that haven't been restored may gradually contract our use of "original" from identity to condition. Under the former sense, a Rolls-Royce hood ornament is original if it's the one that came on the car when it was built—or perhaps on another Rolls from the same period. Turn the survivor lens in front of our eyes to a higher magnification and we wonder whether that same hood ornament, even the one fitted to that specific car when new, is rightly called "original" when it has been re-plated. Original in that case means only identity, not condition, because the plating on it today is not what came on it when new.

At a GM car show at the Minnesota State Fairgrounds in spring 2008, there was a 1970 'Vette in an uncommon color. The owner said the shade was originally slated for a prior model year, but Chevrolet discovered a color-match problem with touch-up paint prior to production and pulled it. He then said a prior-year Corvette had recently turned up that actually was painted that shade; its paint code identified it as a "pilot" color.

How exciting! And this car is in good, original condition? "Oh no," he responded. "It's getting a total restoration." They're repainting it? "Yes," he said. "In the original color."

Under traditional restoration ideology, this is a logical move: take that rare car and make it perfect. To the diehard unrestored-car fan, a one-of-a-kind specimen—or at least its one-of-a-kind attribute—is effectively being destroyed. The car's owner is focused on *the fact of the thing* (the car was painted in this shade) over *the thing itself* (the paint). Once that unique paint,

- Reconstructed title, titled as a 1
- Beautiful original truck
- Frame-off restoration
- Ruckstell axle
- Electric start
- New tires
- Original 4 cylinder

The degree of originality described here is less than that in a vehicle with its original paint, tires, fabrics. . ., like the '59 Fury in Part 2.

sprayed on that vehicle alone some forty years ago, gets stripped off, the only surviving paint job of its kind has been undone. The replacement is new paint. It may look like the original once looked. It may be identified by the same paint code, but it's likely twenty-first-century paint, mixed and sprayed by today's equipment and employees in a modern formulation beside other shades for vehicles that did not exist when that 'Vette was built. The pilot-color car had probably faded, and that was the rub: The original paint was no longer its original shade. Such are the ambiguities and challenges of preservation decisions.

Even when used for identity, the issue of "original" parts is interesting. To be the car's original mirror, must it be the very one fitted by a factory worker on your car during initial assembly? Or is a different one from the same source manufactured the same year still original? If the part was not numbered to coordinate with a particular vehicle, establishing whether it's the exact one originally fitted or an identical contemporary may be both impossible and pointless. It would seem significant only if the one originally installed had some other attribute of uniqueness, such as custom, one-of-a-kind styling or a mark like a driver's or customizer's initials. Otherwise, if even the top experts in the field can't tell whether it was initially fitted to your car or taken from one produced seventeen VIN numbers later, how important is the difference?

Given the passion in this area, someone will pay more for the all as-fitted car than the one with a mirror and a wheel from an identical contemporary, but how would you know, without some unique mark, if what you paid for is what you got? "Knowing" it's the original piece may help us sleep better, even if the proof comes down to belief.

Another interesting wrinkle on originality is that people's memories are fallible as to what has and has not been redone. When you talk to an owner about a very original car and he or she rattles off what has been replaced, quite frequently one or two more changes pop up if you go and have a look at the car. You peer here and there and shoot some photos; the owner gazes

This advanced flaking looks pretty rough. Which would you want, one like this, one replated, or an identical one in its original finish from another '29 Chrysler?

and appraises with you, and often pipes up with something like, "Oh, and I replaced the seal around the windshield—that was leaking" or "I repainted the overflow bottle too" or "one wheel had seized spokes and was out of true, so I found another just like it. . . ." These don't come off as admissions of some prior duplicity; they're just things the owner forgot about. Maybe it's human nature to overestimate the qualities we most admire.

Old Old Joins New Old

The grass is always greener on the other side and opposites attract. In other words, we admire what we don't have. The vehicles at Pebble Beach, with all the money and skill leveled at them, have pushed the concept of beautiful, pristine automobiles to its highest levels. As remarkably difficult as it is to bring

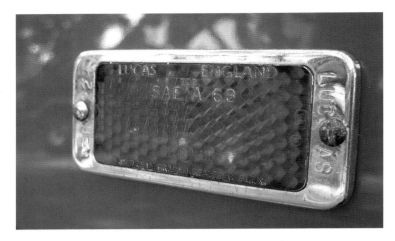

A 1969 MGB GT is fitted with front and rear side reflectors. This is the rear one and is an original Lucas piece. Whether it's original to this vehicle or another '69, however, is impossible to tell without a unique serial number linked to the car.

cars to these standards, you can only make a fender so straight, a gap so even, chrome, nickel, and brass shine so brightly. A point comes beyond which the naked eye can discern no higher level of perfection in fit and finish. Fill a pleasant greenway with such vehicles and even among the history, the variety, the uniqueness of the genius behind these automotive milestones, they begin to exude a certain sameness.

Plunk a car down in this environment with faded, stone-chipped paint; pitted windshield; worn seats, shift knob, pedal pads, and grab handles—a car that looks as old as it is—and a few people are going to say, "Hey, look at that!"

Money is no small force in the car hobby and it works from the bottom up, as well as from the top down. People with the means to buy what they want are expanding their wants to include original, unrestored cars. Those with less disposable income have also played a critical role here. Young people drawn to older cars don't have the money for the flawlessly restored, like-new example. Their budget allows only for cars in less than perfect condition. Naturally, they're going to seek the best example they can find of that sort. These are the good, unrestored cars. Younger fans will buy such a car, get it running and drive it for its style, without seeing it as merely the foundation for a later, sweeping restoration. These hobbyists are kin to the new generation of hot rodders using what they can afford and find, which is no longer 1932 Ford stuff but other years and models. Creativity and budget have turned the rat rod into an art form with no limit on creative uses for new parts, automotive, tractor, farmyard, and other.

The world's supply of older vehicles is diminishing. The skills and methods of yesterday's automotive crafters vanish with them. Saving the mechanical "document" that immortalizes their talents and techniques is one of the driving forces behind preserving and celebrating unrestored vehicles.

As soon as you break loose the fasteners, strip off the finish, yank off the upholstery, scrap what's faded and cracked, and replace it all with new coatings and parts, the car's historical record is blurred. Was that wooden dash gloss finish or matte? Were there lockwashers, or not? Engine bay was body color or black or something else? Hard line where the two colors met or soft? What were the original seats stuffed with? What fasteners held on the upholstery? What hose clamps did the builders use? Rubber lines on the washer system or synthetic? Black or clear or an amber shade?

You can refer to another car like yours, but only if that one is unrestored. Think of the humble Chevrolet Vega. It was too humble, it turns out, so most of the ones that remain seem to have V-8 power. Lots have been built up for drag racing. If your first drive, first date with your spouse, or first time owning a vehicle happened with a Vega and you want one just like it to have and to hold, where do you look for an originality reference? What can you rely on?

Cars that remain just as they were built are the best evidence of correct specifications. Written history is valuable, yet the proof is in the pudding, not the recipe. Consider the 215 V-8 General Motors built in the early 1960s, then sold to Rover in England. All the widely available information indicates that this engine was used in production models (Buick Special and Skylark, Oldsmobile F-85 and Jetfire, and in more limited quantities, Pontiac's Tempest) from 1961 to 1963. It's a hot-rod trick to take the aluminum cylinder heads from a 1964

Buick 300 V-8, with their larger intake valves, and bolt them onto a 215.

Little known are the 1964 Buicks fitted with the 215. Conventional wisdom holds that the 300 V-8 replaced the 215 that year—and overwhelmingly it did. Yet the occasional 215-powered '64 Buick Special does surface. One of these Specials, in the metal, is the best proof that this little-known variation was built. Unrestored, it can also show how it was built, with what fasteners, finishes, materials, and fittings throughout.

Appreciation for unrestored vehicles is growing, fortunately, but it isn't a breakthrough idea. There are collectors hidden and known around the world who have tucked away cars just as they found them without checking age marks at the door. Their collections are like reference libraries for owners of the same vehicles in less original shape.

Farmers have been longstanding sources for unrestored vehicles. Wealthy farm owners were among the automobile's most reliable early customers and that occupation's pragmatism served preservation. When cars and trucks aged out of daily-driver services, farmers used them as utility vehicles to haul people and things around the acreage. Keeping these vehicles in perfect cosmetic condition was unimportant. What mattered was that it handle light farm service without problems, so only what needed repair got fixed or replaced. This is the essential barn-find vehicle: a car or truck removed from daily transport and shifted to more utilitarian uses before finding retirement alongside tractors, wagons, mowers, and other implements. Woody fans, including a few discussed in foreword writer Tom Cotter's "barn-find" books, have many tales of cars that hauled folks around the farm before entering long-term storage in a corner of the barn.

Even in more elite motoring circles there have been drivers content to leave time's marks where they fell. Britain's Alan Clark, member of Parliament, was author of *Classic Cars* magazine's "Back Fire" column and a well known classics driver and commentator. Just after World War II, he bought a Jaguar SS

100, leaving the white stripe painted around its perimeter that allowed other motorists to see it, barely, when London maintained blackout conditions to hide from German bombers. Clark left venerated cars unrestored—not in disrepair, but with mechanical function weighted first and appearances last.

Clark wanted his cars mechanically sound, with performance—not looks—resembling the day the car was built. He chafed at comprehensive restorations, which he felt removed a car's authenticity and just as often harmed the car's mechanical feel. His memoirs describe a Rolls-Royce Enthusiasts Club outing in the early 1990s at which another competitor complained that Clark shouldn't be able to run his tatty 1920 Silver Ghost if he couldn't afford to maintain it properly. Clark took satisfaction that his patinaed Rolls ran among the fastest cars at the event.

Interest in unrestored cars in the United States rose in the 1990s. At the same time, cars once considered "oddballs," like four-door Chevy Bel Airs, station wagons, and El Caminos, began to appear and find buyers in unrestored condition. Part of this is a changing of the guard. The younger generation asserts

Not your aunt's Vega. Some models become so popular for modified uses, it's hard to find a totally original example. How many stock Vegas have you seen?

itself both by buying and thereby popularizing what they can afford and also by seeking out some cars with a different look from what the previous generation bought up and trotted out as its favorites. Unusual cars come onto the scene because the most sought after examples are thinning out, but also because excitement generated by prized cars in unrestored condition prompts those of other styles to offer them for sale to see what happens. If the market wants "unrestored," and that's what your AMC Gremlin is, suddenly that characteristic can give a premium to a car previously ignored.

Supply, demand, increased "unrestored" consciousness from programs like *Antiques Roadshow*, and maybe even some good old-fashioned nostalgia at the dawn of a new millennium, have helped persuade car lovers to show off vehicles wearing, rather than hiding, their years.

If the Internet does not yet hold more information than the Library of Congress, it will. Despite its stores, the 'net doesn't readily tell you that some '64 Buicks used the 215 V-8. This date-stamped unique-to-the-215 bell housing proves it.

An Unrestored Car by Any Other Name

People call vehicles "survivors" in classifieds, blogs, magazines, newspapers, eBay—anywhere the talk turns to cars. The verb "survive" by its nature applies to objects or organisms that remain from a once larger group. Phrases like "the sole survivor" or "only four are known to survive" are old standbys for describing rare and obscure automobiles (and motorcycles, coins, stamps, antiques, species, and so on). The term standing alone does not say much about condition, however. If a Jaguar XK120 survived in a California airplane hangar, protected from the sun, humidity, and temperature extremes, it's going to be in better shape than if it survived on a Vermont carport with an old tarp lashed onto it with clothesline cord.

"Survived" implies that it's whole—half a fish has not survived a shark encounter. If only the frame and running gear is there, however, the vehicle didn't really survive, only those parts did. We know from our experience with batteries, fuel evaporation, and corrosion's propensity to fuse metal objects, that any car stored for a long time is unlikely to fire up and run when the key is turned. But since cars are built to run, it's fair to perceive a survivor as a car that runs or can be made to run. To keep that "survivor" look, work that gets a long-stored car running will be sympathetic to the vehicle's age and unrestored condition.

In this book, we use "survivor" to describe a car that is largely unrestored. Very few cars, especially early ones, are no-mileage specimens stored from new and never used, with every conceivable part exactly where the manufacturer placed it. These vehicles do surface—as collector prices rose, people have bought and mothballed Camaros, Corvettes, Vipers, new Thunderbirds, etc. Every few years a '78 Corvette Pace Car emerges that someone bought and never drove with the express purpose of selling it years later at a profit. Unused, however, is too narrow a restriction to impose on the survivor concept.

Unused, stored-from-new cars also lack a dimension valued by collectors, owners, and admirers of unrestored cars: history. Marks come from use and use is the point of an automobile. We

Station wagons are catching on. Each generation likes to carve out its own niche. Wagons, with their ample room and cheaper price tag, have found a following—which will pull their prices up.

love cars not just because of how they look, but because they drive. They transport us, fast, far, with style or aplomb. Every day on the highways and byways exposes a car to perils as small as a bug to as big as a mountainside. To draw from a car the joys of hurling through space far swifter than we can move on our own feet will leave chips, pits, splats, and cracks. We can see these marks as flaws or as proof that the vehicle has propelled drivers and passengers across the landscape and not just slept.

The survivors examined in this book are cars that have lived and aged and show it. Some of the cars in Part 2 of this book are very original, like the 1989 Mustang GT with everything but its original tires, spark plugs, and alternator, and the 1959 Plymouth Fury that has covered some 3,000 miles from new. Most of these survivors still bear the original paint. Not all of them do, however. Because of the surface area involved, original paint has a strong impact on our perceptions of a vehicle. But if you make original paint an unwavering rule, suggesting that the unrestored appeal is lost every time new paint hits the fender—even if a forty-year-old car was repainted thirty years ago—you encourage everyone with a resprayed vehicle to throw in the towel and redo every nut and bolt. That feels too harsh. We like the stories and remaining originality in the resprayed cars, even if the paint is no longer what the factory applied.

As we use the term, survivor cars are inseparable from their history. This incorporates what their makers did to create them, as well as the life they have led since. If Clark Gable liked to drink coffee while he drove his Duesenberg SSJ and his mug left a pronounced brown ring in the car, removing it in the name of perfection would erase a detail unrestored car fans enjoy. The Ferrari Daytona coupe discussed in Part 2 of this book has a mark where the original owner's wife kept a bean-bag ashtray. The fact that the mark speaks of the Frost family, Stan Reeg's impressive neighbors in his youth, makes the car more, not less, valuable to him. It keeps alive the memory of the people who brought this car into his life.

Painting air cleaners, generators, radiators, fire walls, and so on to freshen up the engine compartment likewise destroys history by covering up the finishes the original builders applied. Everything that is swapped out—carpeting, headliner, original radio, manual transmission, sun visors, door panels—homogenizes the car with new pieces made in a different era, and often a different country. These parts move the vehicle toward generic Ford, Chevy, Bugatti, or Ferrari and dilute its uniqueness as a particular car, built on a particular day, with particular components by specific skillful workers.

These grille pieces
for a '62 Skylark are
not new items nor are
they replated. They're
good original pieces
from another '62 that
the owner found at a
wrecking yard.

What's Its Value *to You?*

IDEALISTS GATHER. THEY HAVE A VISION. A car, a name, an image. They will pool genius in design, engineering, business, and marketing, and they will build an automobile. And it will be beautiful. It will be nimble, stylish, fast. What it offers, the public cannot get elsewhere. This car will change things. This car will change cars.

If the idealists are serious and the design is good, capital is there, and the manufacturing comes together, they and their workers, their machinery, parts, materials, and process will lead to fully assembled, functional automobiles the public can buy and employ in all of a car's purposes. If it's the right idea at the right moment in history, the car could become a legend.

The vehicle's time comes, the public embraces it, races it, tours in it, learns in it, and loves it, and years pass. New idealists come with a new vision and a new design. The old car slips from public view as time, miles, wear, and damage thin its herd. Finally its day is gone. The last examples disappear from daily use. Most have been scrapped, reclaimed for their steel, and fashioned into new objects. A few remain in barns and garages, fields and wrecking yards. Some pass into the safe haven of a museum or private collection.

One comes into your hands.

Everything that was done to this car by the factory and the owners before you is there to see, and so are the effects of use and exposure. The leading edges of the hood and fenders and the front valence are chipped by pebbles kicked up on highways

Old motorsports vehicles are on fire with the collector world. This DeSoto Hemi 1960's rail dragster, used into the early 1970s, is unrestored and full of patina and history.

and dirt roads. The paint is faded from exposure to sunlight and buffed thin in spots from decades of polishing. There are scratches around the door locks where years of searching with a key has made its marks. The seat, carpets, floor mats, and visor are more worn on the driver's side, having seen the most use. There are a few small rips, some stains. The weather-stripping has worn and grown feathery in places, the dash is faded, and the rubber has dried up and cracked.

The car in your possession, long passed from regular use, a model remembered with fondness by some and unknown to others, is not perfect. But it looks at least as good as its age. It's complete and mostly original. Other owners of cars like it could learn from the coatings, colors, fasteners, decals, clamps, and precise locations of many of its components. Its condition is as good as many unrestored cars beginning to turn up at classic car shows and drives. It could be made to run well at modest cost and with few changes other than basic repairs and maintenance.

You must decide whether this car will fit in your life "as is," with maintenance, upkeep, and no major changes, or whether its flaws are beyond your tolerance.

THE VALUE DEVIL

In determining what to do with any project, it's natural to consider value. We want to increase or preserve value and not reduce it. Original vehicles in unrestored condition pose some unique value considerations and require thinking and research beyond the typical collector car.

It's hard to argue that a survivor is more perfect than a car with not a grain of rust on it, whose valves and springs, tires and belts, gearbox, heater, brakes, switches, gauges, fan, latches, locks, wipers, and wires work like they were made yesterday. The survivor does not look better in absolute terms. If the restored car was expertly built, the survivor doesn't function better either, though it may have a more authentic feel. Without heeding history or soul, the preserved car doesn't quite measure up—if perfection is the baseline. More and more, it isn't.

Survivor fans and originality devotees are irked by the fact that market values typically rank a totally restored car superior to an all-original unrestored one that has not had all of its years and beauty marks blasted and painted away. Beware, though. Perspectives and values are changing. Not every rotisserie resto-ration is worth more than an original, unrestored car. There are collectors out there who covet the untampered-with vehicle, and they will pay a premium for a preserved specimen that looks and drives like it was a few years old, rather than a few decades.

Perfection is hard to come by, but anyone with the money can buy it. Originality is a commodity that cannot be recreated. The supply of exceptional unrestored cars is necessarily much smaller than the supply of restorable cars, and as collectors move in and begin restoring, the best preserved cars become rarer than perfect restorations. The last known unrestored cars of any desirable marque generate extraordinary excitement. Consider the unrestored 1938 Bugatti Type 57C that sold for more than $850,000 in Connecticut in 2007—a car projected to bring $300,000 to $400,000. The owner kept it in its largely unrestored condition, a primary feature driving his high bid.

When you happen upon a nice unrestored car, like the low-mileage highly original 3.8-liter E-type owned by Henry Pearman in Part 2 of this book, don't solicit feedback from just any appraiser. You need more than an estimation of condition. Collectors devoted to particular marques treasure fine unrestored examples more than the average auction bidder or generic collector of whatever strikes his fancy. Pearman paid well over the typical market value of a 1963 E-type for an important reason: It is the best unrestored E-type he has found in twenty-five years of buying, selling, and driving them. The way it looks and feels to operate cannot be recreated without a time machine. That quality—exceptional unrestored condition—is a potential enhancement to a car's worth largely untracked by traditional valuation resources.

As the NADA guide to classic, collectible and special interest cars notes, very original cars with authenticating documentation going back to day one can enjoy a price premium as much as 10 to 40 percent more than cars without such history. This estimation, too, is generalized for all cars. Uncompromising fans of preserved cars will push the limits to get what cannot be gotten in any other vehicle.

"PERFECT FOR NONRESTORATION?"

Hollywood loves to remake good movies. Usually the remake is disappointing to fans of the original. If something is already good, why invest so much trying to redo it? Wouldn't the film industry be better taking movies with a good premise that somehow missed their mark and remaking them to seize upon untapped potential?

Like films, a lot of nice unrestored cars have been totally redone for the ironic reason that they were in such good condition already. Fans of the marque who are passionate about originality mourn the loss of these cars. (Those who had them restored, conversely, feel like they've done the cars maximum justice, giving them the same look, shine, colors, and wow-factor they had when new.)

The important thing about total restoration is that you can always do it: tomorrow, a year from now, a half-century on. But you can never undo it. Once the original paint, patina, upholstery, chrome, wiring, rubber bits, decals, plastic, and pot metal parts come off and get binned, they're gone.

If you're on the fence about whether to preserve or restore the car, try getting it running right and use it awhile in unrestored form. These cars are gaining, not losing, acceptance. Even shows like Pebble Beach have displayed unrestored cars alongside the world's best restored vehicles in recent years. Amelia Island has added an unrestored class, and preserved Ferraris are well received at the Cavallino Classic in Palm Beach. You will hear the question, "When are you going to restore it?" Answering "never" is growing more popular. You may find that the people who like it left as it is outnumber—or at least overwhelm with their enthusiasm—the folks making old-car conversation by asking when you'll restore it.

Perhaps you know the car is a survivor and have some angst over restoring it, even though you prefer to drive something that shines like new. Because unrestored original cars are rare and decreasing in number, yet increasing in value, you might consider looking to trade your nice survivor for a rougher, yet complete, example of the same car (or something equally interesting). Restoration experts often advise buyers not to pay near the high end of the spectrum for a car they plan to restore because all the things that give it extra value will be redone anyway and the difference is wasted money. Completely tearing down the body, interior, and running gear and rebuilding or replacing every imperfect item costs about the same, whether what gets scrapped is decent or in bad shape.

If you trade a survivor for a car clearly in need of restoration, you can demand some cash along with the car. A survivor is drivable, showable, and enjoyable in its current state. It has historic value. The car that must be restored to run and drive with a measure of comfort—so you're not sitting on exposed seat springs looking at gauges hanging by wires—is inherently less appealing in its current state and less valuable. The worse off the other car, the more you can ask in cash for your nice one. That amount would help defray your restoration costs substantially if you find the right collector eager to preserve your car in its current state.

Restoration shops understandably like good cars to start with because it keeps their goal of perfection—in terms of gaps, panel fit, etc.—in closer view. Yet the car you trade for might be as straight as your survivor, and if it isn't, that's why you've gone to a good shop: They can make it right. There's no mourning when a car clearly in need of restoration gets one.

Keep in mind, too, that restoration is a very expensive undertaking if done properly. If you pay market value for a car, then pay for a complete restoration, your total costs will exceed the restored car's reasonable resale price. Put another way, unrestored car valuation does not leave a large gap for restoration costs that fit in comfortably below the price of a fully restored car. Collector car ads are laden with vehicles whose owners spent more on them than they are now asking. Consider that fact carefully as you contemplate how to proceed with a nice survivor. Selling a restored car for more than you paid originally doesn't mean much if you lose money overall.

Opting for a "quickie" restoration on a nice survivor is the worst course of all. A cheap paint job and an upholstery kit won't fool anyone into paying top dollar. Knowledgeable buyers will see it as a car in need of restoration and won't shell out a premium for the hasty work. The slap-dash resprays that flourish during market runs wipe out survivor cars and make money only on unsuspecting buyers.

For the best unrestored cars, a shift in perspective may be overdue. Rather than "perfect to restore," consider whether the example you've managed to acquire is "perfect for nonrestoration."

The underside of this lens from a repainted TR6 has a strip of green on it where paint crept in along a tape line. There are small traces to the right too. A slap-dash paint job can ruin an original one without a worthwhile rise in value.

How Rare or Unique?

The first chapter opens contemplating three one-of-a-kind cars—the Chrysler Norseman, Lincoln Futura, and James Dean's Porsche Spyder. These cars sank with a famous ocean liner, were transformed into one of the world's most recognizable TV cars, and killed a movie icon, respectively. Their post-production experiences are so significant, they overshadow the cars' initial conditions.

Cars connected to a famous person or event are worth more than an otherwise identical vehicle. It's where the car has been or what it has done that gives it extra value. Restoring a car like that can be counterproductive, not just for the history lost but potential dollars too. Gun owners who restore a rare or unique firearm often discover they have damaged or even destroyed its collector value, leaving them with a "shooter" that happens to be old.

A good restoration firm will do research before advising you on a restoration. A really good restoration shop will even advise you not to restore if they discover that the car is unique and that its unrestored condition makes it more significant and desirable than a blasted, resprayed, replated version. If you stumbled upon Dean's wrecked Porsche unawares and took it to a shop that realized its identity, the shop's best advice would be not to undo the wreck even though telling you that puts them out the price of a total restoration.

For the extremely rare or unique vehicle, like the unrestored 1911 Oldsmobile Limited Tourer that sold for $1.67 million at a Vintage Motor Cars sale at Hershey, Pennsylvania, in 2007, or the Ferrari 166 MM that went for more than $1 million, the price can be extraordinary even though the car shows all of its years and, in the case of the Olds, is far from few-year-old condition.

WHAT'S THE PLAN?

The best approach for your car depends on your plans for it. If it's display only, you can display a worn car, even a tattered one, as easily as something shiny and crisp. With unrestored cars growing in popularity, restoring something you're only going to admire as art, rather than as a driver, may not be your best use of the money—especially if people will find it just as interesting or more so in preserved condition. Restoration is always an option. Reversing it never is.

If you want to drive an unrestored car that isn't currently running, what will it take to make it run? The original engine, freshened up, does not make for a restored car. Most stored cars need some engine work to run and not break. Yet that work can kick off the slippery slope phenomenon. An owner wants to fix up a scratch, then decides to paint the whole fender, but blending that encourages spraying some of the hood and the door, so why not paint the whole car? If you're painting the outside, how about the engine bay too? While the engine's out, may as well rebuild it, repaint it, and polish it up. If it's going to be off the road, makes sense to redo the interior as well. What starts with a scratch repair, ends with a body-off-frame restoration. The survivor owner would just touch-up the scratch, affecting one square inch of the surface instead of the whole car.

Touring presents some different challenges. Modern hot rodders enjoy the looks of older cars but want late-model performance and safety. Given the tens of thousands of hot rods on the roads, some survivors have gone that route. The owner of a nice survivor who wants to drive the car regularly and on trips has a few options. Assuming the car is capable of highway speeds, one is to brave its age: carefully assess the drivetrain, brakes, bearings, tires, belts, hoses, exhaust . . . and make sure everything is in top functioning order, repairing as necessary. Then pack up your bags and throw caution to the wind. Make sure you have a towing rider on your insurance or with an automobile club and build the possibility of a breakdown into your trip.

There may be some reversible changes you would like, too, like an electronic ignition conversion. Radials will be preferable to bias ply tires. You may wish to fit a third brake light—hot rod suppliers can set you up there. If there are lots of changes you'd like to make, what you're really after is a hot rod or custom. This sort of customization often becomes like a full restoration except that different, more-modern parts get fitted on the rebuild. If that's your plan, and much of the original finishes and components are headed for the waste bin or a parts sale, perhaps a different car would serve your purposes better. As with someone seeking an original-style restoration, you might consider trading your nice survivor for something rougher plus cash to get going on a hot rod or custom project in which you will scrap many of the original parts.

Or maybe the goal is vintage racing. There may be classes for which you could fit some appropriate parts to improve safety

A few tools and supplies are reassuring, and occasionally handy, with an unrestored car.

and handling and keep the originals on a shelf. The more original the cars, however, the less aggressive the competition, typically, to account for vintage-car values and the cars' reduced capabilities and safety provisions compared to modern machinery. If the car already is a vintage race car, you must decide whether you want to push it and risk its fate on the track. For a very original and highly valuable race car, it may ease your mind to build up something less original to throw around, keeping the rare car for calmer, less risky outings.

A survivor's value to you depends on what you want from it and how close to, or far from, that goal the car is presently. Because survivors are growing in popularity and value, it's wise to investigate what the car is worth to collectors focused on your vehicle. This you can do by checking online and live auction results, visiting forums devoted to your car, and referring to

The dealer's window sticker is a great way to show that the car you're presenting today is still equipped as it was when it was sold.

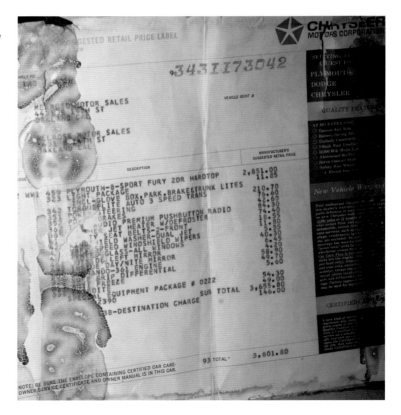

touchstone publications in the hobby like *Old Cars Price Guide* and *Hemmings Motor News*, keeping in mind that the best unrestored cars are setting new high points for value.

If it's the vehicle's style that matters most to you, not its fine original condition, perhaps another example of the same car would be a savvier move than stripping down and redoing or modifying one whose faults as an original vehicle are few. A trade plus cash rewards you for the survivor's condition beyond "restorable." Restoring a nice survivor punishes you for the additional value gutted, stripped, and blasted away in the restoration or resto-modification process.

Not only does the original window sticker confirm that this Fury came with dual-jet windshield washer and variable speed wipers, it shows that they were extra-cost items in 1963.

CHAPTER 4

Preserving What You Have

EVEN THE FEARLESS KNOW old machinery has its limits. Will it break down? Where? When? If Murphy's Law holds sway, the answers are "Yes. Miles from the nearest service station. In rush hour traffic in a hailstorm." Waiting for that breakdown, sensing it will be maximally inopportune and devastating, can drive cautious owners of older cars to tear down every suspect part and renew it, or throw them out altogether and put in some modern running gear.

The trip could end quietly—sputter, wheeze, nothin'—or a steering system failure could suddenly yank the car down a path other than the road in our darkest rest-stop imaginings.

It isn't just functionality that's under duress, either. Older paint jobs have seen years of environmental stresses that have beaten them down, and that's where there's coverage in the first place. Some manufacturers were careful about their priming and paint, and others were more concerned about appearances and getting product into the stream of commerce to bring money back and keep operations afloat. Even a well-maintained vehicle whose unseen steel surfaces are poorly protected can fester with rust.

Are unrestored car fans helpless? Do those who don't own one ask others to drive vehicles in a condition they won't brave themselves? Is the only way to preserve automotive heritage over the long run to redo the paint and mechanicals every few decades?

Preservation does not require restoration. It's possible to address mechanical and deterioration issues in a more focused way. Technology that was once adequate to propel cars across the country still is, if properly looked after. Also . . . *shhhhh* . . . it can be helped.

The term "twenty-footer" describes a car that looks good at a distance but whose faults become more obvious the closer you get. How the body looks is integral to our initial impressions of the car's worth. The hobby's increasing interest in unrestored cars represents an adjustment to this perception. People are crowding around vehicles that have some fading, some checking—cars that wear their history on their finish. Maybe a quest for the unrestored car is to be a good "two-footer."

What if you find an original unrestored car that starts and runs fine and would make a huge splash with your friends and at car gatherings except for one unsightly ding or rust patch? Twenty years ago such a flaw was no big deal because the car was a restoration prospect from the get-go. Today, fixing one small problem is viable. History is an important thread in the survivor fabric. The car got bumped or scraped or something caustic got onto one spot; such things happen to vehicles used to move people and goods and pets and *stuff.* If you fix the ding or the one rust spot as inconspicuously as possible, you keep the car original and mostly unrestored. Collectors of this type of vehicle understand and accept that such repairs are sometimes necessary. Unrestored race cars may have been fixed dozens of times in this as-needed, where-needed manner. It's not much different from any other work except that the goal for the finished look is old rather than new.

The key with the focused repair, rather than the sweeping one, is to maintain the authentic look, not to perfect the repair area. As soon as modern-day smoothness and shine creep in, you can't blend the repair with the rest of a "lovingly used" car without stripping and painting the whole thing.

Many of the cars appearing as unrestored have had some work here and there, both in the past and recently to make them run right and fix any emergency problems. The difference is that that work is approached with an eye toward authenticity,

keeping the fixes subtle rather than making them a shiny standard the rest of the car won't meet.

The body shop's challenge when repairing a modern car
is to match the paint on the repaired area with the rest of the
car. It's not economical to paint the whole vehicle every time a
fender gets crumpled. With an older car, the challenge is more
difficult because the fading is more pronounced; moreover, the
type of paint and the manner in which it was applied differ from
the materials and equipment today. To match old paint, you'll
need a test panel and lots of trial and error to get close. You may
need to spray it on thinner and rub each coat to keep it from
building up and looking fresh, deep, and lustrous. The top coat
will likewise need to be rubbed down to keep it from looking
"too good."

How far it's reasonable to go in keeping a car's old finish
by making complementary old-style repairs varies by car and
owner. Hollywood has paid body shops and painters throughout
its history to create looks of all degrees of perfection, age, or
damage. Top restoration shops are equally capable of inventing
ways to complement lots of nice "old" with a little restorative

This '73 Barracuda had a little rust developing behind the wheel wells. Rather than repaint the whole car, the owners got the rust fixed and repainted up to the bottom of the side stripe, a good eye-tricking place to transition from new to old finish.

new, though it's harder to make something look good up close in 3-D than it is on a movie screen. You may have to talk to a few shops to find one that appreciates your goal of an isolated match of imperfection rather than bodywide perfection. Once they're on board, they can turn their expertise to your purposes, duplicating the effects of wear and fading to suit the surrounding bodywork, trim, upholstery. Trial and error and expertise at this level will not be cheap. Paying big dollars to keep a rare and valuable car in original restored condition will be easier to justify to your spouse than spending comparable dollars on something more common.

What we're talking about here is preserving an authentic look, not trying to cheat someone. As in any market, we can expect rising interest in unrestored cars to create pressure for more of them. This will encourage some people to reach for rougher and rougher cars to dress up or combine and sell at a survivor premium. The restored-car world is familiar with vehicles cobbled together from authentic bits and pieces and offered for sale as lost rarities. A few preservation fans have even commented that unrestored cars can't hide new parts like shiny fully restored ones. Not yet, perhaps. The best defense against trickery is documentation to prove a given car's authenticity along with documented survivors against which to compare new market arrivals.

Preserve Form with Function

Maintenance and careful repairs to promote longevity are not and should not be branded heretical to the survivor concept. Engines, particularly on older cars, are an important case in point. If we are to have old unrestored cars out in the world operating for us all to enjoy, they must run well and not jeopardize the car, driver, or bystanders.

Mechanical problems can be addressed with a non-restoration mandate. Restoration means blast, grind, and polish like new. The unrestored approach allows disassembly, removing meaningful rust, applying lubrication, and fixing structural weakness in the most subtle way.

To keep old, unrestored cars on the road and use them with confidence requires going through all the critical systems and getting them to work properly. A spate of failed brakes and blown engines and breakage-related collisions would do to unrestored cars' popularity what fatal crashes did to races like the original Mille Miglia: brand them as too risky for continued acceptance.

Taking a prewar car, making it run, then driving it hard until a rod goes through the original block does not further preservation. This is why old engines can be found in restoration shops with their cases uncleaned on the outside, yet with new rods and bearings and crankshafts lying on the workbench awaiting some machine work that will make that engine run well for years to come. Maybe the oil pump will be modified for better flow and pressure. Oil galleries may be enlarged or rerouted.

Such unseen changes and improvements are likely to remain soft-spoken details of the survivor world. Unrestored original means things haven't been wrenched on or replaced—making old machinery long-lived and safe, however, requires a little wrenching and replacement. Function controls form: If people can't get the enjoyment they seek out of their cars in unrestored condition, they'll restore them. Of course there are a lot of show-winning restorations that likewise don't get used because the car is too nice to risk it suffering a chip or scratch. Keeping it so unrestored that it's not dependably usable is no more helpful for people who like to drive their cars than over-restoring it to the point of non-use.

Retaining the old look but updating where safety and longevity encourage change is a logical, even laudable, compromise. If you buy an unrestored car to drive, check it out well in all the essential areas. To serve you well, it must start, run, drive, steer, absorb bumps, and stop predictably and with confidence.

A car either starts or it doesn't, but that alone is not a good test of dependability. When a car falls out of regular use, rust frequently develops in the gas tank. Left long enough, it will rust through and leak and that will be simple to detect. But a degree of corrosion less than a hole can leave rusty scale in the tank that's just waiting for a chance to clog up your fuel line and leave you stalled at the roadside. One option is to drain the tank into a light-colored container and look for traces of rust. Check the fuel filter for the same symptoms. If the carburetor is not working properly, you'll want to rebuild it. If you discover rust inside, the tank is suspect. Replace or clean out the fuel line along with other affected parts if you discover rust anywhere in the system.

Check the points, plugs, rotor, distributor cap, and plug wires and be sure everything is within spec and working well. If you decide to replace something, or even fit an electronic ignition conversion, keep all the original parts. As you replace worn out components, you can retain high originality by using new old stock parts (old parts that were manufactured long ago but never used) rather than modern reproductions. The Internet has made such parts and their suppliers easy to find. Various vendors around the nation have been buying out old parts stocks and have stockpiled many obsolete parts. A part manufactured at the same time as your car will keep everything period correct.

In addition to ignition parts, make sure the belts and hoses are in good condition: supple and uncracked, not frayed or bulging. Set the belt tension as directed in the factory manual to avoid slippage. Change the oil and filter, and swap out the air and fuel filters if they look dirty. If either is original to the car and rare, consider storing it, taking proper care in the handling of toxic and flammable chemicals. Set the timing and carburetor adjustments for optimum performance. Drain the cooling system and look for rust in the drained coolant. Pressure test the radiator for leaks. If the radiator's a goner, you can re-core what you have or check wrecking yards for a correct period replacement. A website like www.car-part.com may come in handy for a nationwide search of yards.

With the car on the ground and stationary, push and pull the steering wheel in and out; also attempt to lift up and push down on it. Play indicates wear or loose connections. The steering wheel should not have excessive rotational play either.

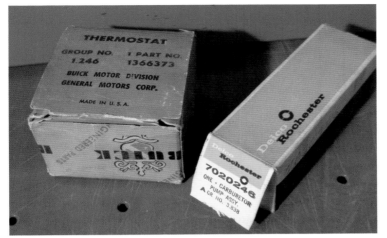

New old stock parts are the very same ones the dealership and factory used to maintain your old vehicle during its daily-driver days. For authenticity, they can't be beat.

Jack up the front of the car and turn the steering wheel lock to lock. Roughness in this motion indicates wear. Likewise check the steering linkage and suspension for signs of wear or looseness. Now check the wheel bearings for play by grabbing the road wheel at top and bottom and rocking in the vertical plane with the wheel off the ground. Motion indicates wear in a wire wheel, bearings, kingpin, or suspension joints. Engage a professional if you have any concerns about diagnosis or repair.

Check the brake pads, brake lines, and their fittings. If the brakes haven't been bled, get that old fluid out of there. Corrosion in calipers and cables is common and will lead to sticking brakes and related problems. If the car will not roll on a mild incline in neutral, one or more brakes are suspect. You can also check for a sticky brake by touching each of the wheels after a leisurely drive. A stuck brake will heat up the adjacent road wheel. The '62 Thunderbird in Part 2 of this book blew a tire because a stuck front brake generated so much heat.

A test drive should reveal wheel alignment or suspension issues through problems tracking straight, thunks, bounciness, or jitteriness over bumps.

If you plan to push the car's abilities, such as through vintage racing, you'll want more than a layperson inspection. In that event, have a professional technician inspect the car. Magnafluxing or x-raying critical front-end components to check for cracks is a good idea. Likewise, check driveline parts to ensure that they are capable of handling brisk acceleration. Check out stressed parts to prove durability or replace them with high-strength items. Ed Godshalk had a machine shop recreate critical high-stress parts on his 1925 Amilcar, featured in Part 2, in hardened steel. (Naturally, he stored the original parts.) He left the car's unpreserved looks intact, while likewise ensuring his continued safety and the car's. Wrecks ruin cars and owners.

What about tires? Original tires fetch good money. Running original tires separates the amazingly unrestored from the largely unrestored. Old tires don't last as long or drive as well as modern radials, however, and are comparatively easy to swap on and off. If you're trailering the car to show off its remarkable originality, then keeping the originals fitted makes sense. For driving pleasure, however, remove and store the old tires and run old-styled radials. Modern tires will ride better and offer better traction, and, unlike your vintage doughnuts, they can be replaced.

If it's a convertible and the top is shot, you can look for that rare unfitted original and bid into the stratosphere if it appears as an auction item. Some collectors will commission custom tops made to look old. The third route, if available, is to buy an after-market reproduction and trade dryness and shade for a measure of authenticity. Old tops very rarely survive except under ideal environmental conditions and modest use, so a tattered soft top is not reason to abandon a survivor as too rough.

Most any system can be rebuilt, repacked, or reoiled without making the outside look new. Such unseen improvements make your unrestored vehicle last longer, and no one's going to take apart the car to learn your secret. It's refurbishment for preservation's sake.

PRESERVATION STANDARDS

Quantifying uniqueness is challenging at best, illogical or oxymoronic at worst. Survivors appeal because they haven't been redone; some marks and wear showing history and use remain. Approaching them from the restored-car perspective where the least flaws are worth the most points is inherently contradictory. It's the "flaws" that make survivors what they are. For this reason, preserved cars suit exhibition classes best, where they vie for crowd appeal rather than judges' points.

The rarest and most unusual cars in the collector hobby frequently wind up at the Pebble Beach Concours d'Elegance, established almost sixty years ago. This exclusive show features two classes for unrestored cars: Prewar Preservation Class and Postwar Preservation through 1967. What organizers are seeking are cars that have not been restored in any way apart from standard maintenance, such as engine work or new tires. There isn't a detailed specifications list further elaborating the requirements. Like many of the premier shows, Pebble Beach is by invitation only; the organizers choose the cars that they feel best represent the show's theme and featured marques for that year.

Another approach to unrestored-car status is Bloomington Gold Survivor certification, developed for unrestored Corvettes

These new old stock tires from the 1950s add a killer look to this rat rod, though the owner admitted he felt a little guilty using them. You can always mount two sets of wheels, using radials for longer distances.

There's a difference between the spotless new vehicle you can buy today and an unrestored car that has shared in your life: one is a conveyance; the other is family.

in 1990. Under this program, Corvettes (initially) were reviewed in specific areas by marque experts who then certified their authentic unrestored condition. That program is expanding to include other marques. Bloomington Gold Survivor certification brings more specifics to the otherwise vague concept of the unrestored car. As explained on their website, to achieve this certification, a car must pass a road test and then demonstrate authentic unrestored condition inside and out. The certification requires that the car be more than 50 percent unrestored and unaltered in at least three of four areas: exterior, interior/trunk, under the hood, and throughout the chassis. In addition, more than 50 percent of the original finishes must retain factory color adequate to serve as models for cars being restored.

Because every unrestored car is unique, the pleasure it brings its owner and onlookers is its most important characteristic. The growing interest in this area will bring more unrestored cars onto the public stage and encourage owners of these vehicles to keep them much as time has left them. How they are discussed and valued will change, as will the way people repair and maintain them. Still, their preservation will benefit all car enthusiasts by keeping alive what the cars' makers created. These cars, and the adventures had in them, are our most valuable sources of automotive history.

Part 2

Survivor Tales

Ami, Ed Godshalk's 1925
Amilcar, emerged from
a Massachusetts barn
to an enviable life for an
antique car—running with
peers in events like the
Mille Miglia. Most older
cars have been stripped
down and made gleaming
approximations of their
early selves.

CHAPTER 5

Mon *Ami*, the Survivor: Ed Godshalk's 1925 Amilcar CGS

IN AN ERA OF BIG, BRAWNY, AND FLASHY, small, modest, and understated stands out. An unrestored 1925 Amilcar CGS, with its faded paint, spindly wheels, tall narrow stance, and long high fenders, is uniquely magnetic. No fan of the hobby seems unmoved by Ed Godshalk's determined little sports car. *Ami*, as his daughter dubbed it, strikes everyone as a four-wheeled friend.

"The car has an uncanny appeal to a wide spectrum of viewers," Godshalk says. "Harley guys like it. Guys in old pickup trucks like it, and women love it." At a gathering where every member of the fairer sex approached the car with a smile, Godshalk asked why they were so drawn to it.

"It's small and cute," one woman replied. "It looks like it needs our care and affection."

Yet faint of heart *Ami* is not. Robust drivers are equally supportive. The Mille Miglia's organizers heard about the barn-find Amilcar and invited Godshalk to run it a thousand miles through Italy's hilly countryside, ancient cities, and cobblestone streets. Racing hero Sir Stirling Moss, who has spent a lifetime in and around fast machinery, singled out the French-made curiosity at Pebble Beach in 2006, discussing it at length with Godshalk among dozens of fully restored cars.

Even famous collector Miles Collier, with his vast knowledge and experience, homed in on the petite boat-tail roadster. He spent about a half hour with Godshalk looking over the CGS and learning about it.

Ami's tiny size is part of its appeal. Godshalk stands six feet, one inch and had an adult male navigator on the Mille Miglia. To

This "voiturette" has not looked like a new car since it was one. Here, early owner Harold Craver and a fellow enthusiast pose with the CGS circa 1926. That's probably Boston's Charles River in the background.

fit two men, Amilcar designers offset the passenger seat, placing it six inches back from the driver's position. This approach allows the men's shoulders to overlap instead of colliding and tilting the occupants outward in cartoon fashion.

Small dimensions make up for a small engine. The side valve four-cylinder displaces 1,100cc—less than many modern motorcycles. But the CGS weighs only about 1,250 pounds, a figure Godshalk confirmed on modern truck scales. Good power-to-weight was a design criterion, essential to Amilcar's numerous racing victories—even in the 1920s manufacturers knew that competition success spurred regular sales. An Amilcar won the world's first twenty-four-hour race, and the marque had some 200 class wins in hill climbs in Britain and continental Europe in the 1920s.

Most appealing to Godshalk is the car's condition. There's no confusion here over what body parts are fresh reproductions and which were made between world wars. If TV's *Survivor* was about unrestored cars instead of contrived small-group dilemmas, *Ami* could be a star. This Amilcar's story tracks with legions of car fans' dreams.

Harold Craver was the earliest known owner of this Amilcar CGS (No. 15514, engine 618, Duval body). Three photos exist dated April 10, 1927, showing Craver with the car in Boston,

Massachusetts. Craver was also a Bugatti owner and a letter survives in the American Bugatti Club archives referencing his association with Amilcars.

Quintin Seail of Westin, Massachusetts, acquired the car sometime around 1940. He put it into storage around 1947, apparently due to minor mechanical problems, allowing the car to remain in a highly original state. Sheltered from rain, snow, direct sunlight, and prying eyes and hands, *Ami* slept in that spot for the rest of Seail's life. When he died in 1997, his seventy-two-year-old lightweight sports car emerged to the light of day for the first time in half a century.

Fate had a particular buyer in mind, but it would take patience. Godshalk, who likes art deco architecture, first learned about Amilcars from a friend on the East Coast. With its upright stance and long, vertical lines, the CGS strikes Godshalk as the quintessential art deco automobile. He had looked at a previous one, a rough specimen offered on a pallet for $7,000. He passed on it and the car went to England. Yet he told the seller, a classic car vendor, to get in touch if he saw another one. A few months later the seller contacted Godshalk regarding the Amilcar from the Seail estate, but an impending

Economic shifts and pressures changed the marketplace later in the century, but before World War II, many enterprising individuals took a shot at automotive fame and fortune. Amilcar was a competent manufacturer with impressive motorsports accomplishments. This is a badge of honor, as well as authenticity.

Appreciation for unrestored cars is rising, rapidly. Prestigious shows are bastions for flawless restorations; in recent years, they have welcomed cars showing their ages—like *Ami*.

trip to Africa to climb Kilimanjaro nixed the purchase. So he let the car go, a decision that frequently returned to gnaw at him.

Most such chances come round just once, but this connection was meant to be. A year later, in 1998, Godshalk found a fresh ad in *Hemmings Motor News* reciting the details still clear in his mind of a highly original Amilcar that had been in storage for decades. He was on the phone and on a plane in rapid succession. A man name George Davidson in Louisville, Kentucky, had answered the first ad, yet the purchase was as far he got. Other priorities had pushed the car off into a corner.

In Davidson's collection, there were several restored classic cars, including another Amilcar CGS. They brushed past

The road wheel and tire have an age-appropriate look, though Godshalk has gone through and ensured brakes and bearings have been returned to excellent condition and performance.

Godshalk's gaze like shirts when you're shopping for shoes. "I went right to the relic," he says. "This untouched ancient car wearing its old paint. It had so much character." There was no passing on the car this time. With joy and relief Godshalk bought the one that got away once.

When the car arrived safely in Oregon, he showed it to a friend who likewise loves cars. "When are you going to restore it?" he asked. Godshalk was as surprised at the question as his friend was at the answer: "Never."

A well done restoration makes an automobile look like the day it was new. Godshalk cherishes his Amilcar looking like the day it was old. Yet preserving the car, and enjoying it,

What matters to Godshalk is performance and structural integrity. Breakage and active corrosion are problems he addressed for safety and soundness. Patina, however, gets left as is; Godshalk loves this car's history and wishes to show it and share it.

meant more than doing nothing. To the contrary, he went to great lengths to retain the vehicle's original, time-tempered looks while ensuring that no fatigued or rotted part critical to the car's—and his own—survival left a weak link to fail on the road.

There was no question that he would drive this "voiturette"— the best way to honor yesterday's fine craftsmen is to use their handiwork as intended. Besides, Godshalk loves to drive. The thrill of taking his cars out on the roads is his reason for owning them, even the old ones.

From 1999 to 2004, Godshalk rebuilt the car but did not restore it. He went through it from the ground up, leaving appearances be, while ensuring that everything worked properly and safely. In every case where the original part was functional and strong, he left it unchanged.

As an engineer himself, such work suits him perfectly. His profession helped him appreciate the innovations the French had employed in 1925. "It's really first-rate engineering," he says. "Their engineers were as fine as we have now. . . . People sometimes called Amilcar 'the poor man's Bugatti' (another marque Godshalk owns), but in some ways it's a better car, striking a good balance between performance and reliability."

He cites the brakes, a component that posed a problem for early automotive engineers engaging them via cable or rods:

How do you keep brake pressure consistent at the front wheels when the wheel-to-chassis distance changes as the wheels pivot around their axis of rotation? Amilcar's solution was to pass a lever-actuated rod through the kingpin. With the rod and the wheel pivoting on the same axis, the distance from the actuating lever to the brake lever —and therefore the braking force exerted—does not vary. The design worked perfectly, and some references cite that both Ford and Alfa Romeo licensed it from Amilcar.

The steel used in the body and frame is also high quality, Godshalk notes, though he replaced critical fasteners in the suspension and steering with hardened-steel duplicates of the original pieces. He could have simply used modern nuts and bolts in the front suspension, but that would violate period correctness. Instead he found a precision machine shop willing to do a small run of pieces identical to, yet stronger than, the originals.

He also had Leydon Restorations in Pennsylvania go through the engine, fitting a stronger crankshaft and rods to handle the Mille Miglia run. "Nothing was harmed," Godshalk notes. All original components are safely stored and could be refitted at any time.

Even with the strong emphasis on originality, Godshalk has no regrets about these changes. "It would be irresponsible to run the Mille Miglia with a stock motor," he explains. And who can stomach blowing up a vintage engine? This was not hot rodding for modern horsepower but selective uprating for durability and preservation of the numbers-matching engine block.

You might guess that such safety-based improvements would include replacing the headlights with new items for greater brightness, yet this speculation incorporates a false premise. Godshalk got the original lights re-silvered and discovered that when returned to original specs they cast as much light as many modern headlamps—just another example of Amilcar's engineers impressing a professional peer the better part of a century later.

Leading a prewar Alfa through ancient streets is an excellent answer to the question, "What will you do with an old car like that?" Leaving such cars unrestored is a further salute to their capabilities and durability.

Given that the car's originality held so much appeal, Godshalk could have left it just as it was. Rather than rebuild and selectively bolster critical systems, he could have returned it to blocks and made *Ami* a static display.

Perhaps that's where a survivor car parts ways with a survivor chest of drawers. The latter gives pleasure primarily from the way it looks; storing clothes there as opposed to some-

where else adds little more. But a car frees us from our bodily limitations to go darting across the landscape at superhuman speeds. A sporting car's looks—while wildly appealing in many cases—can never fully displace the way it feels turned loose on a quiet stretch of road.

The Mille Miglia has been the ultimate test and reward for this octogenarian speedster, one Godshalk videotaped en route with help from his friend and passenger, Dan d'Almeida. The thousand-mile rally through Italy celebrates the famous race of the same name, run from 1927 to 1957 by the fastest cars and drivers of the day. It is the contest Enzo Ferrari called the world's greatest road race.

Although no longer a test of all-out speed, the modern Mille Miglia continues to draw some of the finest vintage racing machinery, including Alfa Romeo, Bentley, BMW, Bugatti, Ferrari, and Mercedes-Benz. Most of the cars have been restored to new or better than new condition. *Ami*, with its faded, weathered paint, imperfect brightwork and overall untouched feel, stood out like a genuine time-traveler—a visitor from a distant

Paint is the first thing our eye is likely to catch in appraising a given car's condition. More than eighty years on, the Amilcar's finish has faded and flaked. Poor old thing—about all that's left for it is having the best drive of your life through the countryside!

You can't get more vintage feel than this steering wheel provides; no one will ask if it's a reproduction. Details make the difference—just one Phillips-head fastener in the dashboard would ruin the period look.

future returned to the original race when the event was young and thriving.

Crowds rightfully love every car that runs in this demanding rally today, reviving sights and sounds that drew motor racing's greatest names to this country for thirty phenomenal years. Yet like rare survivors often do, the Amilcar drew a special sort of attention, so starkly and unabashedly bearing the years that were polished and painted to extinction from most of the other vehicles. Officials from the International Federation of Antique Vehicles (FIVA) inspect each car to ensure authenticity. They gave the Amilcar an A2 rating, the highest originality rating on a car still in active use.

Peering out the Amilcar's two-pane windscreen—wider at the top than bottom, the car's little four-banger singing away through a reedy side-swept exhaust, Godshalk feels he was meant to be at the wheel of this car. His five years rebuilding it—painstakingly preserving the original finish while commissioning hardened spindles and bolts to upgrade safety and main-

tain looks— and the work he did with Chris Leydon, keeping the motor original in appearance and function while improving durability to modern standards, fills Godshalk with joy. The car lives on in its remarkable survivor status only because it found its way into his capable and caring hands.

Ami is a true survivor, a piece of history to see, touch, hear, and drive. Few owners would have left the car looking as it did when it emerged from a Boston barn after fifty years on blocks. They would have "improved" it with a sweeping facelift. But to engineer and auto-history fan Ed Godshalk, the marks the decades have left upon his voiturette are the very features that make it shine. The decades' patina is more resplendent than any coat of paint modern crafters could spray.

These are original lights, re-silvered to handle night driving. Unrestored condition is important to Godshalk, but not when a part left as it is would put car and driver in jeopardy.

Whenever Henry Ford had questions about the best way to assemble his cars, he would turn to Gene Hetland for answers, or so this poster suggests. Hetland's garage is surrounded by blown-up photos of the Ford factory. His wife, Patricia, modified this one, putting Hetland right there with ol' Henry.

CHAPTER 6

Deuce Heaven— Gene Hetland's '32 Fords

As a teenager in the 1950s, Gene Hetland had one thing on his mind: Fords, particularly the '32. Oh he had girls on his mind, too, but if you had a car in high school, getting a date wasn't much work.

Hetland never cared much for school. He wanted to be working on cars, or at a job useful to that interest. His cousin had lent him a copy of *Rod & Custom* magazine in 1954. The hopped-up '32s on those pages inspired him to buy his own when he was just fifteen. He stored it at a friend's welding shop. There was no room for a car at his own house, though—and he didn't have a license—so Hetland got rid of it. But the shop provided some welding skills he could use for repairs and fabrication.

He has fond memories of those times and the friend whose father owned the welding shop. That friend, Daryl, added some thrills and stories to Hetland's youth as well as helping with his Fords. Daryl liked to offer his views to people, especially those whose opinions of themselves were higher than Daryl's estimation. He was a football player, stocky, so he had some power to back up his mouth.

One evening Hetland and Daryl were out cruising in Daryl's '40 Ford when they came upon a carful of college kids. These guys thought they were a big deal and Daryl disagreed. He offered some of his own observations on them and their car. The college boys followed them, which was fine with Daryl, though Hetland was less enthusiastic about it. They tailed the '40 Ford back to Daryl's house and leapt out to teach the younger men some respect. Daryl grabbed the nearest guy, picked him up over

This '32 Cabriolet not only wears its original paint but also has four original tires and its original top. Restoring an original car in this fine undisturbed condition would substantially reduce its value.

his head and threw him against his garage door. "He crumpled to the ground like Beetle Bailey," Hetland remembers, and they all took off. Hetland recalls chasing after them as they fled. It was nice having a tough friend.

Another time Hetland was the passenger while Daryl was driving a '53 Ford dump truck across the bridge between Fargo, North Dakota, and Moorhead, Minnesota. They got behind an old woman whom Daryl felt was driving too slow. So he put the dump truck's bumper against hers and helped her accelerate to what he felt was a reasonable speed. It's doubtful the woman appreciated the free horsepower, but no harm came from it.

"We were mischievous," Hetland says. "We didn't drink or smoke, though." They were young people bending the rules, a phenomenon some towns addressed by giving kids better things to do. One such activity was drag racing, which Hetland and

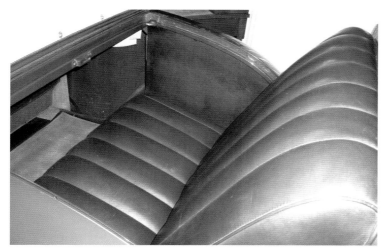

This rumble seat still wears its original fabric; condition is excellent. This car was stored for many years in a private museum before Hetland acquired it.

friends did at a strip near Fargo-Moorhead (as the two towns are collectively called). Hetland had a '40 Ford of his own that moved out pretty well and furthered his appreciation for the flathead V-8. What he really wanted, though, was another '32—his vision of automotive styling perfection. "There's nothing finer," he says. "There's nothing out of place on a '32. Every line has a character to it that's made for the car."

The first Deuce he could actually drive he scored in 1957. It was sitting in the back of an implement dealer's lot—a farmer's trade in. The car still had its original motor, which Hetland promptly pulled with a friend and swapped for a later-model flathead; at that time, his focus was performance, not originality. He ran that car hard, followed it with a '34 Ford and then another '40. Racing ate rubber, but it wasn't a problem back then. "We'd go to scrap yards and get tires," Hetland recalls. "They were yours for the taking." The yards had to get rid of them and didn't mind young people gathering them up for free.

Wrecking yards were also full of Ford parts, which he and his friends learned to swap out and fix up. "There were thousands of old Fords back then," Hetland says. "And almost no old Chevys or Plymouths. They didn't last." The few that did made little impression. Hetland and his hot rodder friends were all about the flathead V-8.

The paint has a few thin areas from decades of polishing— classic patina.

In addition to his periodic car and speed parts purchases, Hetland accumulated new old stock Ford components, which was easy because dealerships wanted to get rid of them. "Every town had a Ford garage," he remembers, "and they were plumb full of old parts because Ford never took them back until the 1960s. All the little Ford garages either had an attic or a basement full of parts." He remembers visiting a place in Ada, Minnesota. The man told him that a guy from Minneapolis had come and bought a whole truckload, paying what the garage had paid for them new in 1932! The garage owner thought this was a good deal for himself, while Hetland felt the other guy got the best of that one. He happily paid '32 prices for his own batch of parts that he bought to resell. "I paid $2.50 for a '32 fender," Hetland says. Bet the dealers that sold off those parts wish they had a few now.

Selling old Ford parts cheap wasn't the most surprising way Hetland found dealers getting rid of them. In the late 1950s he went to a scrap yard and saw men laying out new old stock '32 fenders, running boards, and grilles and driving over them to smash them flat. With his reverence for the'32, Hetland was horrified at the destruction and the wasted opportunity. He knew a man working at the yard and offered to buy the parts that were still good. The yard worker responded that he'd get fired if he sold any of it. They came from a large dealership outside the Twin Cities and the dealer didn't want people to fix old Fords; he wanted them to buy new ones.

Yet Hetland's heart stayed with the old iron. He and his wife took their honeymoon in a '40 Ford, then moved to the city, Minneapolis, "to make it big." Building on his experience from the welding shop, and another job sanding and shaping metal at an auto body shop, Hetland landed a position at a metal stamping business in the city. "I've found heaven," he thought. Metal stamping was a job he enjoyed and that offered further skills and insights for car work. After a while, he realized "anybody can do this, and I could do it better than the place where I worked."

Knowing he could improve upon his employer's products, Hetland decided to start his own metal stamping company. It took a while to develop the business, so while he waited for revenues to build, he sold off '32 Ford parts to keep food on the

The adjacent Roadster is another very original car, sporting its factory-applied paint, top, and interior. You really can't lose with a '32 Ford. If it's very original, it has high value for that reason. If the car is rougher, or less original, there's a long line of hot rodders eager to buy and transform it.

The door paint shows wear from regular contact with hands and forearms. This Roadster top shows a little dirt but is not damaged.

table. He also parted with an engineless '32 three-window coupe he'd bought to tinker with before he went out on his own.

Yes, he'd started his business to make a living and feed his family, but he also wanted to succeed so that he could pursue his Ford hobby. Any nice Ford gets a second look from Hetland. He owns a Mustang GT and World War II–era Ford-built Jeep, as well as several woodies. All have a place in his heart—just a smaller place than those from '32. He also has collected a lot of interesting Ford automobilia, from original dealer posters and signs, to experimental parts, to curiosities like Ford brand charcoal briquettes (which Ford invented) and Ford fertilizer and Portland cement. Much of this side merchandise derived from by-products of the company's manufacturing processes.

Hetland has one of the signed paintings of Edsel Ford that dealers had during the years Edsel ran the company. Edsel also features in one of Hetland's few race cars. Speed legend Harry Miller built Edsel an open-wheel car that ended up in the hands of a wealthy Detroit man. This man liked all things fast and fell

Original rumble seat is in good condition; the Cabriolet's is so extraordinary, however, that it makes this one look rougher than it is by comparison.

in love with a hooker he saw on the street. He decided to get her out of that situation, offering the dangerous men who controlled her $5,000 for her freedom. The men accepted the offer, took the money, and then took the man's life, cutting him up, so the story goes, and scattering his pieces around the city. People lost track of the car until the man's widow sold it years later. Unfortunately, it was tucked away so long those people who would have known the car during Edsel's time had passed away. The car's known history is consistent with the Edsel car, it is fitted with appropriate period parts, including many custom-made items, and Hetland has old magazine photos showing Henry's son at the wheel of a car identical to the one in his collection.

The small-town kid who came to the city to make it big is retired now, devoting most of his time to his growing Ford collection. The '32 count stands at about seventeen today, and includes several extraordinary unrestored examples, as well as some of the finest restored cars. His collection includes four roadsters, three three-windows, one cabriolet, one five-window, one two-door, one Victoria, one four-door, one pickup, one station wagon, a roadster pickup, a phaeton, and a sedan delivery.

Hetland knows these Fords inside and out and can tear down and rebuild most any system on the car. Because of his extensive

This grille has a few blemishes but is not bent or otherwise damaged. Replacing it with a flawless reproduction or replating it would be a mistake on this car.

History and proof of use is what separates the restored from the unrestored car. This '32 two-door had a conscientious original owner who recorded on the car itself all of his maintenance work. This is the door frame; when he regreased wheel bearings, he wrote those particulars inside the hubcaps.

metal-working background, he can also fabricate many of the parts he needs or wants, from mounts and brackets to custom headers as fine as any custom header shop can build.

His cars needn't be unrestored and they don't need flathead power, either. He's a fan of the five-liter engine, and has a '32 woody with a Harry Miller four-cylinder. Still, when outstanding unrestored examples surface, Hetland doesn't wait to pick up the phone. "You always have the dream of finding that special car," he says. "If you hesitate too long, they're gone."

He keeps in touch with the scene through his many contacts from the Ford hobby. "If you get to know old cars, you meet a lot of nice people. . . . Most of my friends aren't in this town," he adds. They're spread out in many states. Hetland likes to fly

Modern paints are tougher than the nitrocellulose lacquer applied in 1932. Here's another spot where generations of washing and polishing have rubbed through the finish. It's patina, though, not damage, as the panel is not rusty—just rustic.

out and meet his '32 buddies at swap meets. "My wife [Patricia] calls it 'male bonding.' She enjoys that I do it." When friends are in the Minnesota area, Hetland will tell them, "Why don't you stop by and see my latest toys."

All of Hetland's closest friends understand his devotion to the Deuce, which keeps him looking at or working on them every day. Once, he was talking with some visitors and mentioned maybe taking a vacation. One of them responded, "You don't need to go on vacation. You've got paradise right here."

"If you're into the hot rod . . . ," Hetland explains, "we live and die for '32 Fords."

Tom Porter says this is not
Minnesota's fairgrounds,
but it may as well be. This is
what the No. 111 car looked
like in its racing heyday.
These cars had no starter,
so a push truck got them
going before a race.

Old-School Speed:
Tom Porter's '23 Model T Hot Rod
and '54 Kurtis-copy Midget

IN THE FIRST GRADE, Tom Porter got to sit in a race car owned by Twin Cities hot shot, Red Lempelius. That's all it took for the racing bug to bite hard. Driving race cars was a natural extension for a guy whose skills and interests ran toward mechanical things. These abilities surfaced in high school, where his sharp eye and steady hand caught the shop teacher's attention. He asked Porter how many hours of shop a week he was taking. When Porter answered, he asked if he'd like to double them. Yes, he would.

Porter set up and maintained the metal lathes and milling machine and became adept at using all the tools in the shop. After school he became a mechanic, making sure some of that wrench turning went into race cars. His first year on the track was 1966, racing a '46 Ford coupe in the hobby stock class. His

TOM WITTA

Tom Porter worked for Twin Cities engine builder Tommy Adelmann, taking over the shop when Adelmann retired. He has acquired, raced, tuned, and built a variety of cars, including Adelmann's 1923 Model T Hot Rod (built in 1946) and Midwest midget racing champ Howard House's car.

Adelmann raced the 111 car hard and successfully before taking the running gear for a sprint car he built. This body tub, seat, and many other parts went on a shelf at Adelmann Engine. Porter has rebuilt the car with original parts or proper period replacements.

father came to two races, in both of which Porter rolled the car during warm-ups. His father was done, but Porter was just getting started. He continued to hone his craft, adding modified, sprint, and late-model cars to his resume.

When he and wife, Karen, had kids of their own, Porter got them into racing too. Sons Brian and Alan raced quarter midgets. Brian's is a genuine Kurtis, which he drove very well. At age six or so, he was too small to reach the controls comfortably, so Porter gave him three inches of Styrofoam on top of the seat and in front of the backrest. The padding and the Kurtis worked well: photos of his kids holding racing trophies are as prominent around the Porter home as shots of more famous cars and racers that Porter has met during his tenure driving and building racing and street engines.

His own time at the wheel did not go as smoothly as his sons' time, however. The thrill of racing is also the risk. It's dangerous to move way faster than fixed objects, like track walls or piled-up competitors. In 1971, Porter was running a sprint car at Northstar Speedway, in Blaine, Minnesota. Suddenly the driver ahead of him hit a dry spot in the dirt and spun. Porter emerged from the dust and saw the car about the same time he hit it. The collision cost him one kneecap and took him out of work for months. One less kneecap didn't stop him from racing, however. He kept with it for the enjoyment and experience and won a few heat races along the way. He still drives with the IMCA (International Motor Contest Association) Old Timers for some more regulated fun at speed.

After a dozen years repairing all automotive problems, Porter took a job with Tom Adelmann to focus on building and rebuilding engines. Lots of great stuff came into the shop and the old-school methods Adelmann used keeps bringing them in. Parts, charts, and service manuals from the 1930s and before still take up shelf space. There are rings, bearings, gaskets, and other goodies that most folks haven't even heard of in their original boxes. Every so often some of that stuff still gets used. The shop takes in engines from the brass era to last week. Whether iron or aluminum, push-rod or overhead cam, if it burns gas, Porter works on it. About the only things he usually avoids are air-cooled and diesel engines. The shop is an institution on the local vintage car and racing scene.

Adelmann was well known in Twin Cities racing circles both for his driving and his professional skills. In the 1940s, he saw a 1923 Model T roadster in a farmer's field—of which there were many in Minnesota at the time. He pulled into the farm, inquired about the car, and cut a deal with the farmer. Restoration was not his plan. Racing was.

He stripped the car down, scrapped the four-banger, and had a local fabricator roll the roadster's body edge down smooth and reinforce it around the cockpit. Left-hand steering went away in favor of a centered wheel backed up by a war-surplus bomber jump seat. Some 1930s wire wheels, quick-change rear end, and a flathead V-8 with high-compression heads, dual Chandler-Groves two-barrel carbs, and a Mercury crank put power to the

TOM WITTA

ground. As a professional engine builder, Adelmann knew all
the speed tricks of the day—and they worked. His white Model
T racer, marked "111," bested the field in the first hot rod race at
the Minnesota State Fairgrounds in 1946.

Adelmann kept the car and the trophy at his shop as unbeat-
able advertising for his services. In time, as was the trend, he
pulled the bodywork and built another racer with the rolling
chassis. He kept the parts, though, year after year and decade
after decade. When Adelmann died in the late 1980s, he passed
the shop and the 111 car on to Porter, who rebuilt it with original
and period parts.

Today the first hot-rod victor from the venerable state fairgrounds is reassembled with the same body, gearbox, rear end,
heads, intake, carbs, and surplus jump-seat, that Adelmann put
ahead of the pack more than sixty years ago. Porter sourced a
Model T frame, flathead V-8 (of which he has many), and the
same style of 1930s wire wheels. The paint on the car is the very
coating from the 1940s, right down to the door numbers and
the versatile moniker "Tommy" on one corner. Apart from the
unique body, the cylinder heads may be the rarest parts on the
car. In all his years specializing in flatheads, Porter has seen only
one other pair like them, hanging in the background in a magazine photo of a speed shop.

Whatever Adelmann didn't transfer over to the new car stayed with this one, including the World War II-surplus jump seat mounted in the center of the cockpit. This is a pretty hot piece of custom paraphernalia; rodders today still make knockoffs of the real deal.

In addition to the 111 car—and some other collectibles, like a right-hand-drive steel-wheel Austin Healey 100-6, and race cars, including a pair of small-block-Chevy-powered sprint cars—Porter owns another well-known Midwestern race car. Anybody who raced midgets from the 1950s to the 1970s knew Howard House. Drivers got to see the back end of his number 12 cars as they charged to seven championships between 1960 and 1979.

Porter's car is a (Frank) Kurtis copy that House built in 1954, to which the future midget champion transferred a Ford V-8 60 from his first car. In 1960, House swapped out the little flathead for a straight-6 Ford Falcon engine and the car came into its own. House took the midget championship in Kansas City that year, and again in 1961. For several years, he then switched to driving a friend's Offy-powered midget, but climbed back into the number 12 car to win the St. Louis midget championship in 1968. He continued to race it into the early 1970s until it finally ceased to be competitive. In 1973 House sold the triple-championship midget to John Chapman of Springfield, Missouri.

The car traded hands a few times and ended up being offered to Porter's friend, Shorty Ellis. By this time the frame had been shortened by 13 inches and a new hood fitted to cover—gasp—a motorcycle engine, blown (not supercharged). Somebody with

This May 1956 photo shows the first iteration of the Howard House No. 12 midget. The motor in it at this time is a little Ford V-8-60.

no sense, or knowledge, of history had cut the Howard House car down to compete in mini-sprint. Ellis told Porter the price and said he didn't want to pay that. Porter said, "That's a good price; buy it." Ellis did, making plans to rejuvenate the car as House had owned it, but he never got to it. Next time Porter saw him, about ten years ago, he asked how it was going. Ellis said he wasn't doing anything with it and would sell—for the same price he had paid. "You gotta jump," Porter says, when a car comes along at a good price. He could see potential that his friend couldn't.

Though its "new" look was pretty horrid, Ellis had gotten the original front bodywork, which passed to Porter, along with several Falcon engines. Whether one of these was the very one House set his records with, Porter can't say, but he knew he could rebuild the car as House had raced it. He restored the frame to proper Kurtis-midget dimensions, refitted the House front bodywork, and installed a Falcon power plant. Porter had done some engine work for Jerry Weeks, who made an appropriate flaring for a Kurtis midget. He gave Porter a hood flaring that had been in a museum in Indianapolis. Porter incorporated it and then painted the car just as old photos showed it back in the House racing days.

The car has seen a few changes, including a Falcon six-cylinder engine—an upgrade House made, after which he won three championships in the car. The rollbar does the looks no favors, but it allows Porter to run the car in vintage meets, driving being more important than looks. Front shocks have also been upgraded from the car's early years.

The car House built is a Kurtis copy—modeled after designs by primo car builder Frank Kurtis. A key to his approach is the tubular frame. Wheel and dash are not what House had in the 1956 picture, but cars change a lot over the course of a career as drivers add and subtract parts for speed and comfort.

On its first outing it ran slow and Porter knew why: The gearing wasn't right. Next time out he put in gears suited to a quarter-mile track and the No. 12 car ran great on the half-mile: The Falcon engine likes to sing at around ten grand. Porter has driven the House car at least a dozen times in vintage meets. "Once I got the gears sorted, it stuck really good," he says.

Fun as it is, a race car never really ceases to be dangerous and Porter has pushed some limits. "Racers play hard," as he puts it. Two years ago, he and his friend Jake took it out in the parking lot by his engine shop to see how it would run first start of the season. "Fast" was the answer. Enjoying the moment,

One limitation with the classic House car is that it doesn't float. Neither does Porter when he's inside it; luckily he's calm under pressure and got himself and the car out without damage. Only "harm" was a few photos memorializing the event.

Porter came in fast to a turn at the end of the parking lot by the corner of the building. "I didn't have the race tires on the front of it," he says, "I had trailer tires." As old No. 12 started to slide, Porter remembers thinking, "don't jump the curb"—as the car disobeyed. That was a serious problem because of the pond just beyond that end of the lot.

"Don't go over," Porter thought, but the car tripped on the curb and rolled one and a half times, leaving him mostly upside down and underwater. Racing and crashing are part of going fast, however, and Porter kept his head. He stayed still and waited for the bubbles from the splashdown to respond to the laws of physics. When they floated away, he knew which way up was. He exited out the top of the cage and emerged from his embarrassing wreck. As a longtime chum and racing buddy, Jake did what circumstances required: He ran to the neighboring business, borrowed a camera, and snapped a shot of his friend and his vintage race car in a pond. Porter's seen too much of the racing life, with its far more serious carnage, not to laugh it off.

The Howard House No. 12 midget is much as it was forty years ago, though it wears a roll cage now. Because of the car's highly competent Frank Kurtis design and excellent power-to-weight ratio, it is still abundantly fast. Of course, Porter has all the tools, know-how, and incentive to keep it in racing tune. With a busy shop, a family, and grandchild, Porter doesn't get out in the car every season, but when he does, the purchase proves its worth. Along with hot laps, Porter gets to meet racers who remember the car and the champion who built it. One such man helped Porter track down the legend whose name again proudly marks this midget.

Some cars are known by their numbers, some by their engines, some by their sponsors. This is the Howard House car, another piece of racing history to escape track and Time largely intact.

Sure, you could strip off this alligator hide and fit a close approximation, removing the splits along with the authenticity. The posed and racing shots show Dave Garroway on this seat; anything else is just one like it, which anyone can fit to their SS100.

CHAPTER 8

Classic Cats: Henry Pearman's Ex-Garroway Jaguar SS100 and Kin

In England, history reaches so far back an American can easily mistake a building's construction date for its street address. Something beginning with "13" or "14" hardly makes sense in the United States. It's just too old. Respect for what was done where, by whom, and for what, is tradition in England, one motoring fans apply to the country's long line of sporting cars. Among British marques with a proud history, Jaguar runs out front for its unique beauty and accomplishments.

Henry Pearman has hunted Coventry's cat from the time he was a boy too small to reach the pedals. He wanted an SS 100 Jaguar by age eight or nine and had one many years ago. That car was original and unrestored but too far gone to drive or keep as it was. He got rid of it, determined to find a better one when opportunity arose. It had to be a real one, though—a genuine SS 100—not one of the various knockoffs or derivatives made over the decades. In his many years among Jaguars, Pearman has seen period saloons cut down and reworked into reasonable copies. There are also kit-car SS 100s featuring fabricated bodies on more modern running gear. Experience is one way to distinguish the variants; documentation is another. Pearman is plenty familiar with this marque to know what he's looking at, yet like most collectors he also welcomes any documentation prior owners have gathered.

Jaguar's biggest sellers have been the cars that crossed the pond to attract American buyers. The SS 100 found a prominent and capable owner in Dave Garroway, original host of NBC's *Today* show. Garroway raced the car frequently against

A chronometer,
a fixture in period
competition cars,
is mounted in the
steering wheel center.

JAMES MANN

competition that included Briggs Cunningham and he fared well, incidentally promoting the car to a wide audience. Because he was a celebrity and liked speed, the TV star hot rodded the SS 100 with an XK engine and smarted up the interior with alligator hide upholstery way back in 1951, after the original—now supercharged—engine failed.

Garroway's race-tuned roadster was well known to American racing and automobile fans, appearing at the New York

Auto Show in the early 1950s. The car was also featured along with its famous owner in various magazine articles. It may be the best known SS100. Fortunately, the few subsequent owners respected the car, leaving it as Garroway had modified and raced it. The car is not all-original to factory specs, but it remains as modified and customized by its most famous, long-term owner. That combination of famous past and unrestored presentation makes this a highly desirable car.

Pearman picked up the rare cat's tracks a few years ago and the chase was on. The script was the same as for his other race cars: "You learn who owns them," Pearman says, "then you chip away." Rare cars that hit the auction block go to the highest bidder, but only the right person can get hold of one in private hands that isn't actively for sale. Pearman expressed interest in acquiring the car and discussed his own collection and the marque with its then-owner. Within the last year, he crafted an offer that proved irresistible—five E-types and a Morgan Plus 8. The cars came out of Pearman's holdings, which include the largest E-type assortment in Britain.

History was a big part of this car's appeal, above and beyond looks and performance Pearman has admired since childhood.

Oft imitated, never equaled. It's easy to see why *Sports Cars Illustrated* called Garroway's choice the most beautiful sports car ever built. An alligator interior made sure no one had an SS100 exactly like his.

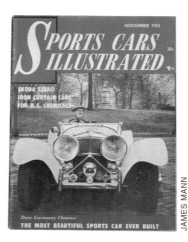

The car is yellow here and the lights are not protected from flying debris. Owner Garroway might be compared to Jay Leno today: a television personality whose interest in cars was well known and followed by the press.

JAMES MANN

After the above photo was taken in 1955, Garroway made some changes to the car. A photo of him and the SS 100 on the August 1959 *Jaguar Journal* cover clearly shows the leaping cat hood ornament in place. The car now features bigger mirrors, plus auxiliary lights, and is white. Garroway may have done some damage at the track or dressed up the Jag for street use.

JAMES MANN

The ex-Garroway car came with boxes of records and photographs from the fast cat's prominent life. He hasn't had the car on the road yet, but looks forward to getting behind the wheel of one so much nicer and more powerful than the one he had years ago.

The SS 100 is a good example of a car valuable for its originality even though the "original" condition is the nonfactory guise in which Garroway owned and raced it. Retaining a car's early character is critical to Pearman's automotive outlook, both personally and professionally. His company, Eagle, E-types, uprates a small number of these cars to more modern

performance specs each year. Yet the upgrades do not alter the car's design integrity. "We won't go with ABS or electric windows," he says. "We just 'put them in the gym for a while.'"

The owner of one of the twelve original factory lightweight E-types sought out Pearman for an interesting challenge. He wanted the car returned to the look it had when the owner saw the car leading a 1963 race at Silverstone, driven by Roy Salvadori. The idea was not to restore the car in the conventional sense, but to take it back in time to that date and color scheme.

Pearman and his crew got lucky in their quest: They managed to trace the '63 paint color to a particular manufacturer and actually turned up a small amount of the original pigment. Disassembling the car, they also found traces of the paint as applied to the body. The paint match they achieved was not the color as it looked when first applied, but the same shade as it would appear having aged more than thirty years. This required painstakingly adjusting the formula to achieve a slightly faded, matted down look in paint freshly applied to the aluminum panels. With an authentic paint job in place, the rest of the work involved removing grime but not refinishing

The Jaguar has provided lifetimes of driving pleasure to the car's lucky owners. Henry Pearman is doubly lucky, owning and driving the Jaguars for enjoyment, and sometimes more competitively, and also working on and selling them professionally. The Garroway SS100 is a special and unique prize for his collection.

Rock chips are a heart-attack risk for a trailer-only show car's owner. On this E-type, they're proof that someone has enjoyed this fine sports car on the roads, where it belongs.

anything. "All we did was take the parts off, clean them, and put the car back together." Where a nut or bolt or hose clamp was missing or no longer period, they replaced it with a correct vintage Jaguar part.

There was one "blemish" they were careful to leave in place. After the car's Salvadori racing days, its owner used the lightweight E-type in hill climbs. Forty years ago, she had placed her own "redline" on the tachometer in nail polish. Pearman and his crew left this mark, a singular touch from the car's past that would have been wiped clean in any concours restoration. When they finished with the factory racer, it looked as though it had been in a museum for forty years. Although it took longer and was more difficult to approach the car in this way than to strip it all down and redo everything, Pearman took on the job in part "to prove you can restore a car without making it look brand new."

Pearman's own collection also includes race cars. He's particularly fond of the Group C and GTP sports cars. While the lightweight E-type presented a color question, his own more modern race cars from the 1980s provide greatly multiplied restoration issues. Cars often ran in three or four different liveries over a single season. One of his Porsches ran in six. A race car's last race before retirement isn't necessarily its most prominent, the one for which collectors are most interested in it. When Pearman gets a car that was retired following an unexceptional performance, he sometimes chooses to reproduce its look during its moment of glory.

Accomplishing this goal requires a detailed study of photos and footage of that race to determine the exact paint scheme and logos in place at the time. The trick then is placement. Pearman says the numbers or logos are often applied by someone from the crew, such as a mechanic. How square they are and where placed depends on which mechanic stuck it on there and how fast. To get it "right," Pearman pays attention to such imperfection. To be true to the car he's honoring, he will find all of the same logos and place them in exactly the same positions, regardless of how straight or crooked that placement appears. The important thing is not that the car look great in isolation;

This forty-five-year-old car has an impeccable interior, as nice as when a typical '63 E-type was two or three years old. Makes sense—the car has only seen 35,000 miles of use.

JAMES MANN

The I.D. plate and surrounding area show a little chipping and fading—one of the few places where the car's originality is obvious. Different rivets or bending or marks at the corners often reveal when a plate has been popped off during a repaint.

JAMES MANN

rather, it's that someone looking at a photo of the car on race day cannot see any difference from the car as it exists today. When Pearman can't tell, no one else can, and that's when the job's done right. He laughs that this may seem extreme, but for a devoted racing fan, details mean a lot.

Along with the SS 100, there is another recent prize in the Pearman collection: the best original early E-type he has ever found. He had known about the 1963 3.8-liter car for years. A sympathetic owner had cherished it for twenty-five years, kept it sheltered, and gave the car only "gentle exercise," using it enough to keep it running perfectly yet produce no performance-eroding wear. The car's paint, carpets, instruments, engine, gearbox, upholstery, and top are all original. "The car drives like it's two or three years old," Pearman says. "The Moss gearbox doesn't crunch. To get one like that is such a buzz." Because of its extraordinary unrestored condition, he paid two to three times the going rate for a restored car of the same period.

This E has minimal travel for forty years of use. Yet it isn't one of these cars showing only a few months of exercise, total, on the odometer. Pearman also owns one of the last E-types made, which had covered 3,300 miles when acquired and, since careful recommissioning, still only shows 5,500 miles. His recently acquired '63, by contrast, has 35,000 miles—few enough to have left all of the well-maintained components functioning

JAMES MANN

flawlessly, yet enough travel that some use here and there won't constitute a dramatic mileage increase.

When he does restore a car, Pearman's goal is to make the end result much like his "new" '63, retaining the vehicle's early character. Restored cars he saw in the 1970s and 1980s were often "glorified resprays," which failed to recapture the car's original feel. Just as restoration can fall short, it can also go too far. "A restored car should reflect how the car was new," in Pearman's view. A forty-year-old E-type with a modern engine or everything in the engine bay triple chrome plated would likewise fail this test. In both cases, the car's essential character no longer reflects what Coventry built and the public embraced with such zeal during its production run.

Pearman prefers the cars that come to him unrestored. In that condition, Pearman says, "a car can talk to you and tell you its history." Obliterate Time's marks and you silence the car's voice, reducing proof of its identity to stories and documents. With many vehicles in Pearman's collection, like the ex-Dave Garroway Jaguar SS 100, that would be a loss, for in those cases, the car's history is as important to value as the car itself.

It would have been wonderful to pen the E-type's lines—yet sad, too, knowing you would never top them. If the SS100 was the best looking sports car of the prewar era, the E-type can go side-by-side with any car on Earth for the same honors afterward. No wonder Pearman went well above typical values for this superlative example.

JERRY LEE

What does Bob
Youngdahl do with
his classic sports
cars? This.

CHAPTER 9

The Pond-Hopping Boano Coupe: Bob Youngdahl's '57 Ferrari 250 GT # 0667GT

IN A LAND OF LIMITLESS LAKES and cold weather, ice racing is an obvious outlet for the restless and the reckless. (The passive and the patient favor ice augers and fishing poles.) Bob Youngdahl was in high school when the green flag dropped for the first sports-car ice-race in the state, winter 1952. St. Paul, Minnesota's Lake Phalen, venue for the event, was just four miles from the school. Watching grown men throw small cars slipping and sliding around a track banked up with snow left Youngdahl with some new ideas about his future. He was going to go wheel to wheel with his peers, and may the best man win.

They didn't use studded tires in the early years on the lake, yet certain risks counterbalanced those diminished by slower speeds. The snowbanks lining the track would stop a sliding car's tires at ground level, pitching overzealous drivers wheels-up. Youngdahl remembers several sports cars rolling in that first race. It was an important lesson: The fastest driver doesn't always win; you have to finish.

Youngdahl had a high school friend whose parents had bought the young man an MG TD. Cruising in that car sharpened Youngdahl's interest in driving and racing sports cars. He watched every road race he could get to in Minnesota and at Elkhart Lake, Wisconsin, along with all the ice races. For one lake event, his friend loaned his car to a very fast local driver, hoping to see his MG take a checkered flag. Instead, he got to watch it roll over; it had been a little too fast for its own good and the snowbanks were as reliable as ever.

As with Cobra owners, enthusiasts lucky enough to own a classic Ferrari tend to use the serial number when discussing the car. With today's VINs that would require a good memory on their part and lots of ink on ours.

JERRY LEE

On winter evenings, Youngdahl and his pals practiced on Lake Phalen. They had no permission to do this, however, and the police would regularly show up to kick them off. Yet law enforcement generally welcomes activities that keep young men out of real trouble, like street racing, drinking, and fighting. Slipping around on a frozen lake was pretty harmless in the grand scheme of things and the cops were tired of breaking it up. Finally, one of the officers gave the young ice drivers a helpful rebuke: "What's the matter with you kids?" he asked. "Don't you know our shift ends at midnight?" In exchange for a little less sleep, the would-be racers got to hone their skills uninterrupted, except for rolling a '46 Olds convertible and an MG TD. Youngdahl didn't roll his '47 Chevy convertible, but he sure bashed his share of snowbanks.

Although he watched the races as frequently and attentively as anyone, Youngdahl did not take the wheel in high school or college. The reason was money. Oh, he could have borrowed some and gone racing with everyone else, but that's not Youngdahl's style. "I knew men who fed their families popcorn so they could afford to race," he says. Youngdahl didn't want debt adding pressure or deleting enjoyment out on the track. So he focused on his career in engineering sales and paid off every creditor, including the mortgage holder on his hobby farm. Now it was time to drive.

While he has the original engine, numbered 0667GT, this is a spare. The insulation under the hood is what came with the car.

To keep abreast of his favorite sport, Youngdahl subscribed to *AutoWeek*, which in those days was a racing paper. It also included classified ads—from the United States and abroad. The year was 1969, by which time Ferrari was known throughout the world as a racing tour de force. The model 250, built in many forms, had become legend. There in the pages of *AutoWeek* was a 1957 Ferrari 250 GT (no "O" at the end; it came later). The car was in England, a pleasant coincidence because so was

JERRY LEE

Bob Youngdahl restored the exterior of his '57 Ferrari GT almost forty years ago. At this distance it still looks great.

Youngdahl's younger sister, who was watching a group of child travelers. He phoned her and she agreed to go to Manchester to check out the car. Unfortunately, on the appointed day one of her youthful charges got sick and she couldn't keep the appointment. So Youngdahl called the seller, who started the car over the phone. From a verbal description and an engine note carried overseas to a telephone receiver, Youngdahl agreed on the deal: $1,900, excluding shipping.

The seller put the car aboard the cargo ship *Manchester Renown* bound for Chicago. Youngdahl took a trailer and headed east with his brother to meet his Italian coupe (built by Carrosseria Boano for the Ferrari factory from a Pininfarina design). They coordinated the pick-up so they could catch the races at Road America on the trip, naturally. At the Chicago dock, Youngdahl and his brother looked over the Manchester Ferrari. The paint was nice and the condition appeared generally good, but the shifter was missing. Youngdahl opened the trunk and found the transmission—or a transmission. The twin-plate Sachs clutch the 250 required was not with the vehicle. He

Youngdahl painted the wheels on the car, which were flaking and starting to rust. The one on the right is a good original. Pirellis are 1960s-era items Youngdahl bought from a fellow racer.

JERRY LEE

and his brother tried to start the motor. It wouldn't go at first so they primed the carburetors. Youngdahl hit the starter again and a hefty backfire singed his brother's eyebrows. Time to give the startup effort a rest.

Further complicating matters, Customs officials refused to release the shining Ferrari because the seller/shipper had failed to steam-clean the car as the United States required due to an outbreak of hoof (foot)-and-mouth disease in England. (The theory at the time was that the disease could be carried in mud, all of which had to be removed from the Ferrari's wheel wells, underside, and engine bay before it could be moved.) Young-dahl knew what steam cleaning could do to paint and tried to slip a twenty dollar bill to the kid working the machine to go light. Unfortunately, Customs officials stayed close and required the cleaner to go three times around for about twenty minutes underneath the fenders.

Their next setback was discovering Youngdahl's brother's early El Camino wasn't up to the tow job. It couldn't pull the trailered Ferrari more than forty miles per hour without swaying, so highway officials kicked them off the expressway. They stored the car with a nearby friend and returned later with Youngdahl's pickup truck.

With his purchase finally back in Minnesota, Youngdahl checked the radiator. Good thing it hadn't started in Chicago,

This Ferrari never toured as a trailer queen; it's been driven hard and raced, leaving some chips, cracks, and dings. The lenses on these Marchal lamps are getting pricey, Youngdahl says.

there was no coolant visible. He and his brother put a garden hose in it and went inside for a beer. When they came out it wasn't overflowing. Youngdahl removed the oil filler caps and water gushed out. Later disassembly revealed that two freeze plugs had popped out of the block. On the trip across the sea, the *Manchester Renown* had encountered freezing weather, yet the seller had not drained the coolant or added antifreeze. Now the $1,900 Ferrari with its loose gearbox and no clutch needed an engine rebuild.

Did Youngdahl lose patience? He'd been waiting seventeen years for a Ferrari of his own—so no. He tore down the engine himself and rebuilt it. There was no manual available, so he relied on his own mechanical skills and engineering background. After a year's worth of machine work, he put the engine and transmission in the car and tried once more to drive his 250 GT. A quarter mile down the road, the wheels locked up. Ferrari's large double-leading shoe drum brakes were state-of-the-art in the 1950s. Presently, they were seized. Youngdahl managed to free them up enough to get the car back to his shop for a brake rebuild at all four corners.

The following winter was extremely cold—Minnesota cold—with temperatures well south of zero and below what Italy and England experience. It was too much for the steam-cleaned paint that had looked so good at the Chicago harbor. The once smooth nitrocellulose lacquer was falling off in hand-size flakes. That seventeen-year wait for a Ferrari was getting longer. More than a few cars get sold for failing to cooperate on this scale. For Youngdahl, the situation just meant the car would be that much more a reflection of his handiwork. He was not an experienced body and paint man. Yet.

Youngdahl stripped off the disintegrating red finish and learned more about his purchase. He found seven layers of paint in four different colors. Fortunately what lay beneath was in good shape; there was only one small body-filler repair to the left front fender. The damaged area was as good a place as any to start refinishing the car. Youngdahl began with the driver's fender and worked his way around the car, sanding and smoothing the door, roof, and trunk lid. By the time he got back where he started, his skills had improved. His initial efforts were

Apart from the early racing belts and the fire extinguisher, the interior on the car is original. Black leather seats show their years, but are otherwise in nice shape.

Being a GT, the car could be ordered with fitted luggage, though touring isn't why Youngdahl bought it. Magnetic racing numbers are about all that's been behind the seats for four decades and the carpet still looks good.

JERRY LEE

no longer up to snuff, so he worked his way around again. After two laps, the panels and gaps were as good as he could get them. A couple of quarts of Ferrari red and this car would turn heads on every block.

A private collector friend active in the Ferrari Club of America had some good—and interesting—news. He had a paint code which, according to urban legend, derived from a Ferrari owned by one of the GM brass. This man and a colleague walked by his car one day and decided that they'd like to license that color. They contacted Pininfarina, but the Italians refused to cooperate. So the GM exec brought out his paint people and told them to analyze the color, which they did with modern spectrometry. The paint experts said they had it, so the executive told them to paint his car with it. As the legend continues, there was another Ferrari in the executive lot with its original red. After the paint job, they parked the two cars side by side and the derived shade was identical. That paint code is the one Youngdahl got from his friend. He applied nineteen hand-rubbed coats to his '57 250 GT.

With the mechanicals and the finish restored, it was time to have fun. Beautiful body work or not, that Ferrari was going onto Minnesota's Brainerd International Racetrack. Youngdahl was now racing both winter and summer. Not one to go halfway,

Built for driving, the 250 has friendly controls, with adjustable-length steering column and lighting stalks angled for easy reach from the wheel.

he helped start a vintage racing organization to bring additional venerable cars out onto the track. He campaigned the Ferrari in road races in the vintage class; he wasn't going to fit a roll cage and make the other safety changes that would significantly alter the vehicle.

His rebuilt coupe could move. There were a few well-tuned Corvettes that could pull away, but mostly his Ferrari ran toward the front. One race day morning at Brainerd, he glanced at the dash and saw what no driver wants to see: no oil pressure. Youngdahl cut the engine, coasted through a corner, and turned into the paddock. Engine failure was a dismal prospect but at the moment he wanted to race. His son, Bob Jr., was also at the track in Youngdahl's wife's Jaguar XK120. Youngdahl had sold that car long before to buy his then fiancée a wedding ring. Later, when the buyer needed some cash, he was able to buy it back, presenting it to his wife as a wedding anniversary present. When he announced that he was taking the car from Bob Jr. that day in Brainerd, his wife had some news for him: "No you're not. That's my car and Bob Jr. has been practicing in it, and he's going to race it." Instead of the driver's seat, Youngdahl settled for a color-commentator chair in the announcer's booth. His son finished well and Youngdahl was able to navigate his commentary with a racer's

JERRY LEE

The car arrived from Manchester, England, with the gearbox in the trunk. Although 0667GT has always been left-hand drive, the shift pattern is reversed. Youngdahl has many cars and occasionally lets other drivers take the wheel, so a diagram helps avoid destructive errors.

precision, staying out of trouble even though he would rather have been driving.

After the event, he met a man with a spare 250 GT engine. Youngdahl figured he would need one, so he asked to buy it. The other man was willing to sell, but Youngdahl had to take everything—the '59 coupe, plus the engine. Youngdahl agreed to the deal and the family headed home. After work the next day, he took out the manual he had since acquired and checked out the oiling system. There were two things downstream of the oil pressure regulator: a remote oil filter and the gauge. On a hunch, Youngdahl pulled the regulator and dismantled it. A chunk of scrap iron was holding the regulator open. The only oil failure his '57 Ferrari had experienced was to the gauge itself.

Despite considerably more work than an *AutoWeek* ad had initially had him imagining, he loved his '57 250 GT and had made a good deal on the '59. He stuck to it and brought that car home. It sat outside on a trailer at his farm into the fall and got blanketed by a big early snow. Youngdahl moved it into the converted granary he used as a shop and let it sit, snow and all.

Ferrari prioritized his gauges. Gas and water temp are useful for road driving but not so critical for performance as to make the main cluster.

The dashboard, steering wheel, instruments, carpets, etc., are just what the factory fitted in 1957. There are not many left wearing their years like this.

Now retired, Youngdahl devotes most of his time to his cars, especially to racing them. Though restored and without patina, this Porsche-powered Elva would leave our feature car behind in short order.

THE POND-HOPPING BOANO COUPE . 117

Racing and extreme temperatures can be hard on auto glass. Like so many other parts on this car, the windows are original pieces.

The engine with a valve-cover off is the original engine for the car, numbered 0667 GT. Youngdahl will swap it back where it belongs. The other is either a spare or the original for the '59 250 GT in the background. The gearbox is for that car.

The winter was another cold one and in the spring the snow was still sitting on it. That car became the Snow Bird. If the '57 took a long time to work through, the '59's been even slower. The main reason is that Youngdahl doesn't need it. He has a perfectly functioning 250 GT already, as well as many other cars that he drives and races. The '59 is getting a show-quality restoration.

Today, Youngdahl's backed off on the ice racing, or maybe ice racing has simply declined to a novelty in the twenty-first century, when most lakes are ringed with homes whose owners don't want midnight drivers honing their skills out the bedroom window. Instead, Youngdahl sticks to the paved stuff, racing in the Midwest and out of Florida during the winter. He races sixteen to eighteen weekends a year and says he has run twenty-six of the forty-six licensed race tracks in the United States. The paint and bodywork he was so proud of shows its age now, having seen a lot of years and miles since he did the work more than thirty-five years ago. The patina fits though, and the car still has its original interior and trim. He drives it when he can and it always draws a crowd. They've been through a lot together, and he has other cars that have taken far less work for the same fast laps. With his first racing Ferrari, however, Youngdahl has no regrets.

JERRY LEE

The brightwork, like everything on this car, is just as it left the factory, including the original Koppy Motors badge. Paint is what Plymouth division sprayed a half-century ago. It shines like a fresh coat.

CHAPTER 10

The Cars Come to Him: Red Leonard's 1959 Plymouth Fury

ALTHOUGH COMEDIAN-COLLECTOR JAY LENO is a legendary car sleuth, he gets offered uncountable vehicles without lifting a foot or phone. When people know you're into cars and acquire worthy examples, they come to you. Such is Red Leonard's good fortune. He's been in the car business his whole life. Automobiles run through his family as strongly as red hair. (Red's real name is Harold, but only family members and longtime friends know it. He's lucky to own the nickname, too, given that his father, mother, brother, and three sisters all had red hair.)

Leonard's father started selling Fords in South St. Paul in 1925. The first time the father took a horseless carriage to his parents' farm in Millville, Minnesota, he offered Leonard's grandfather the driver's seat. Many farmers were leery of cars at first, worried they'd scare the horses. But this family had an open mind. The farmer got in and pointed the huffing Model T toward the road. When he reached the end of the driveway, he yanked back on the steering wheel and shouted, "Whoa!"

Cars were not so easy to stop, as a ride or a profession. The automotive life suited Leonard. He enjoyed the designs and innovations and liked that his family offered a product the community relied on. Back in the day, cars were a big deal, not something every family had two or three of, like today.

New-model introductions had an air of mystery and celebrity. Manufacturers wanted the public clamoring to see the new models, then kept them carefully out of view. They would put the word out before anyone outside the company had a sense of what the new styles would be. Cars were shipped covered on

Red Leonard opened his Minnesota dealership when the '59 Fury was four years old. His sons, Jim, left, and Tom (not pictured), also joined the business. Red points out that none of the '59 Plymouths that came to his dealership that first year was nearly as nice as the unrestored car he got from the Saint Paul man who bought it new.

a transport, enough for highway travelers to get a sense of the lines, perhaps, and want to see more.

Vehicles headed for the Minnesota capital city, Saint Paul, were stored in lockup at the state fairgrounds before they were released to dealers. As a youth, Leonard and his friends would try to sneak onto the property and get an early peek before they went on public display. New model introductions were fancy parties at many dealerships and people would come from distant towns to see what Detroit's gurus had created. The public's enthusiasm toward the automobile left an impression on Leonard. Receiving each crop of new vehicles and providing them to an eager public was a profession that made sense and felt right.

In 1945, Leonard's Ford-seller father passed away. A year later Leonard bought a Dodge. He liked the car's style and ride and decided he wanted to pursue a different line from what his father had sold. His choice had precedent: The Dodge brothers themselves had gotten their start working for Henry Ford before moving on in their own direction. Leonard has a Dodge Touring car from 1914, the first year Dodge Brothers Company built a

If the only damage that leaps to the eye on your fifty-year-old unrestored car is a couple of scratches on a decal, you have something very special in hand. This one is still good enough to serve as a model for a reproduction label.

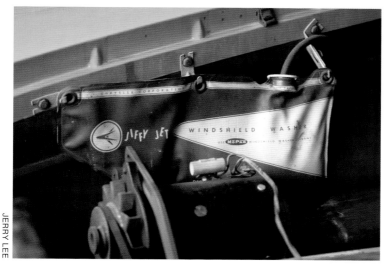

Don't mess around with a Minnesota winter. Thirty degrees below zero, not counting wind chill, happens many times a decade. Leonard's '59 Fury was so lightly used that the flimsy plastic washer-fluid bag never cracked. It hangs from the original hooks on their original bolts, the writing as legible as the day it was made.

vehicle for sale. One of its headlights says Dodge; the other says Ford. It's a perfect car for a man whose life has been bounded by both brands.

Drawn to the Chrysler line, Leonard took a job selling DeSotos from 1953 to 1956. During that time, car dealerships in Minnesota were open seven days a week. He could have taken a weekend off here or there, but those were the days when most people were free to shop for cars. Taking off some time midweek would have been odd for that era, so Leonard hustled DeSotos

JERRY LEE

One headlight—the inner passenger's side bulb—blew. Leonard left it, keeping all four of the original lights in place. The car is virtually never used at night, so swapping in a replacement bulb had no practical value.

every day for three years, then went to work at the Minneapolis regional Chrysler office from 1956 to 1960.

The next rung on the ladder was management experience, which he found at a Chrysler dealership in Rochester, south of the Twin Cities, home of the Mayo Clinic.

Ten years after his first car-sales job for DeSoto, Leonard was ready to own his own Chrysler store. The site would be his hometown of South St. Paul. You might think Fury Motors came from the Plymouth model, perhaps even the car featured here. Not so. The name was just another twist of fate.

For business reasons—easy to remember, easy to find in the phone book—Leonard wanted a short name beginning with a letter near the front of the alphabet. He enlisted his wife's help for brainstorming and she said, "How about Fury Motors?" Perfect, Leonard thought. Plymouth's Fury was a solid, basic car in the Chrysler lineup, but his wife wasn't thinking cars at all. She loves horses in single digits and had offered the star's name from a favorite book, *The Black Stallion.*

Cars are Leonard's life. They've been his primary focus and livelihood, and he's moved thousands of them. Yet some models

had a little something extra, some styling touch or presence on the showroom floor that really caught his eye. Sending cars out the door is business; bringing special examples back in, for keeps, is a personal pleasure.

As soon as word got out that Red Leonard over at Fury Motors liked to buy nice classics, owners of older cars saved their classified-ad dollars and called Leonard first. All of the cars he's collected over the years were offered to him. "I never went looking for my cars," he says. "They came looking for me."

Today that collection includes the 1914 Dodge Touring, a 1927 Model T Ford, 1934 Plymouth, 1954 DeSoto, 1955 Town & Country station wagon, 1963 Sport Fury, 1967 Barracuda convertible, and 1969 Satellite convertible he sold new, then bought back with 100,000 miles on it. He also has a 1941 Ford one-ton truck that his father sold to an uncle. Leonard even has the original invoice with the two familiar names on it.

Several years ago, two salesmen were on the showroom floor when a man walked in and asked, "Want to buy a Plymouth?" "What kind?" they asked. When the man named the car, they realized whom he'd come for. Leonard was certainly interested

The original owner started the car regularly throughout its decades of storage. Leonard replaced only the water pump and, of course, the battery. All wiring, radiator, insulation, paint, decals, hoses, and so on are the original 1959 items. The 318 V-8 ticks over instantly when you turn the key.

THE CARS COME TO HIM . 125

Yes, that's the original mileage. It takes something unusual to produce a car from midcentury last that has seen only a few months worth of driving in all those years. In this case, sadly, it was a serious illness for the original owner's wife. Leonard preserves both the car and its story.

JERRY LEE

Chrysler's famous push-button dash kept transmission controls out of the driver's and passenger's way. But, as Leonard says, people resist change. When Chrysler polled its customers on what they preferred, they voted for a shifter over the elegant buttons.

JERRY LEE

in an old Chrysler product. The car was in Saint Paul, just north of the city of South St. Paul.

The eighty-five-year-old owner took Leonard to a garage with two locks on the small door and a concrete barrier pushed up against the big one. Hidden away in the little building, surrounded by modern roadways crawling with fuel-injected, computer-controlled cars and trucks, in the shadow of skyscrapers with jets from around the world passing overhead bound for Minneapolis-Saint Paul International Airport, was a car unchanged from its first year in existence—four years before Fury Motors opened. The mileage on the odometer is what most cars accrue in their first few months.

The owner, its original purchaser, had bought the car new in 1959. Shortly afterward his wife got sick. The place where she received care was walking distance away, so the car never got used. He thought he should sell it, but she didn't want him to.

Instead, it remained in the closed garage. In its own world, it was and is a new car. But outside time passed, leaving 1959 years and then decades behind.

In half a century of buying, selling, and collecting Chrysler products, Leonard had not seen this Fury's classic equal in originality and low mileage. The car before him was in better condition than the four-year-old cars that came into his dealership in 1963. Did he want to buy a Plymouth? This car was sold the instant he laid eyes on it. The paperwork was a mere formality.

Given the car's history, it's an ironic color: Bittersweet, with creme. It has what Chrysler considered a big innovation at the time, its push-button transmission. The buttons work cables routed down to the automatic gearbox. Leonard says Chrysler offered this shift method in 1956 and thought it would be widely embraced because it took the lever out of the driver's and passenger's way. The company felt it would win out when manufacturers responded to the government's command to standardize shifting patterns to prevent dangerous mistakes as people traded

Gritty soles invariably wear pedal covers after a few seasons' use. Not on this car. As with the upholstery, steering wheel, and every other component, these pedal covers look like new old stock parts with a little dirt from the maneuvering for this photo shoot.

No matter how original a typical unrestored car, forgiveness is always given for perishable items. With this car even that concession is unnecessary. The tires, wiper blades, and brakes are the ones that came on the car in 1959.

Many things find their way into the trunks of 1950s cars, including junk, water, weeds, squirrels, rats, raccoons, and rust. Find a factory photo of a '59 Plymouth's trunk and it will look just like this.

Even when all the trim is there on a classic, pits and peeling can wreak havoc on aesthetics. These dual antennas are perfect—and cool!

JERRY LEE

from one manufacturer to another. Yet when Chrysler surveyed its owners, the company was surprised to learn that a majority of its drivers preferred a lever.

Leonard has many nice automobiles, but none is a better unrestored car than the Fury. Few examples so original and low mileage turn up anywhere. It takes special circumstances for a car like this to go so long in such extraordinary condition. At such times, it's good to be a man people come to when they have a vehicle that's old and unusual.

Today, Leonard is mostly retired but he still goes in to the dealerships. "If you don't like the business, it's work," he says, "but I like it. It's fun for me." When his two sons were young men he told them, "I'll pay for your education and you can do what you want." He didn't push cars on them; he didn't have to. Sons Tom and Jim are third-generation car men, selling Chryslers at two locations today. Jim has red hair, too, like his father. Some things run in the family.

Tom and Jim also enjoy classic cars. Jim is fond of the '67 Barracuda and Tom likes the '69 Satellite. Both enjoy the 1959 Fury, and the dealerships' salespeople have an unspoken under-standing: They're to give Tom or Jim a prompt call if anyone comes in with a question like, "Want to buy a Plymouth?"

A California garage
provides optimal storage
conditions for a pair of
unrestored, albeit once
repainted, Porsches.
The registration on the
red car changed to a
California black plate
in 1963.

CHAPTER 11

Love in a Teardrop: Shiffrar Porsche 356 Coupe and Convertible D

For more than six months, Genevieve Shiffrar's parents, Ruth and Arthur, stored a friend's 1961 Porsche 356 coupe in the family's yard in Fremont, California. Genevieve adored that car. She loved the sensual shape and its unique shade of white—"not bluish white. It's yellowy, creamy white, like milk"—a color that perfectly offset the tan interior.

Her older sister, Maggie, had a '59 Convertible D her parents bought new in 1960. They drove the car constantly, racking up more than a quarter million miles before giving it to Maggie for the best birthday present she ever got, arguably the best possible.

Genevieve was fifteen, toeing the line of driving's freedom. How cruel to bring a car so nice and leave it there in the yard for her to admire, covet, and dream about driving, darting, and downshifting over California's hills and along her stretches of ocean majesty. But there it was, someone else's prize she could enjoy with eyes only.

Ferry Porsche's simple, mesmerizing design is said to have been inspired by a drop of falling water. It's false inspiration, it turns out, for a drop of water doesn't look like that as it falls, only as it's about to fall—yet no one cares. The graceful curves have an earthiness to them, a sense of the basic and the essential. While trim and wheel styles come and go and lock a car's looks in time, aging has hurt the 356 not one speck. If anything, its styling is more compelling than ever.

When the Day of Driving Age arrived, the coupe Genevieve had admired so much was gone. It had moved to the driveway to assume its true identity: as her car.

G. SHIFFRAR/T. GRUBBA

The pleasure of owning her own 356 coupe has diminished a full zero percent since Genevieve got this car as a high school student. The gift was essential in the name of fair parenting, as older sister Maggie had received Ruth and Arthur's Convertible D.

There is justice in treating your daughters alike, but Ruth and Arthur had had complete success in convincing their youngest that the white coupe belonged to someone else. Now the secret was out and Genevieve was stunned, thrilled, and confused all at once. Her father was a truck driver, her mother a teacher. They had raised her to disapprove of flaunted wealth, yet here she was, a girl getting a Porsche for her sixteenth birthday.

If her age when the car became hers still makes her a little embarrassed, it hasn't hurt her appreciation for this fine sporting machine. The Shiffrars had their best friends, Don and Dorothy Britton, over for lunch and Don helped Genevieve learn to drive her present. That afternoon negotiating familiar streets from an unfamiliar driver's seat—learning the gearbox and when to shift and how to use the floor-mounted clutch pedal—is clear in her mind, one of the high points of her life against which all other experiences are unconsciously measured.

The white coupe was original except for its engine and paint. Arthur had a guy working for him in Los Angeles running some

trucks who knew a woman with an inoperable 356. She had broken the crankshaft and was looking to sell. Arthur bought the car and put in a 1600 Super engine. "That was a really fine engine," Genevieve remembers. It was very responsive with a beautiful sound. It's no longer in the coupe, however.

Genevieve's favorite high school teacher had recommended a filmed version of *La Traviata* playing in San Francisco. She and two friends piled into the coupe and went to the show. On the way home, friend Jaime, crammed into the back, had an exchange with the driver.

"It's really hot back here," he said.

"It's supposed to be," Genevieve replied. "This is an air-cooled car."

"No," Jaime pleaded. "I mean it's *really* hot."

When you're young, rolling along on a sunny California day with good friends in your Porsche, things are right—so very right, they cannot be wrong. Genevieve ignored her passenger's protestations until the white coupe took his side. The engine stalled and they coasted to a stop. You could smell the heat.

Arthur arrived and opened the engine compartment. "He pulled out a broken fan belt and threw it on the ground and

Here is the car in its original finish during its early years. Ruth and Arthur Shiffrar drove the car regularly and far, circumnavigating the United States on one trip.

The car's current shade is slightly different and the dual mirrors, set mid-fender, have been replaced by a more conventional driver's side mirror by the A-pillar. Wheels, hubcaps, trim, and most everything else are the same pieces in both photos.

stomped away," Genevieve recalls. "He was so mad—angry at himself because he knew the belt was on its last legs."

The coupe got another engine, not as powerful or refined as the 1600 Super. The car also got resprayed about 1984 in Corvette White. Before the Shiffrars bought it someone had put sound insulation all over the bottom of the car, perhaps in an effort to lessen the wonderful air-cooled purr. It started to fall off and look bad, so Arthur scraped it all off. Though he was careful, this work left a few marks he was unhappy with. A friend of Arthur's painted it, putting on a light coat and rubbing it down, then repeating the process, until the whole car looked right again. The interior, wheels, bumpers, and trim are all original as far as they know. As long as they look good, function well, and do not detract from the car's charm, they will stay that way. Some wear and dirt is expected and accepted.

The coupe exists, at least with the Shiffrars, as a mandatory addition to the 1959 356 Convertible D that Ruth and Arthur bought new in 1960. Porsches came to the family not as a use for surplus dollars, but from a love of sporting cars.

Harsh winters are brutal on cars, but this was a rare exposure to snow for the red Porsche. Good thing, too, given how little of the windshield the wipers clear.

With its perfect weather, unmatchable scenery, and—at the time—vast open spaces, California in the 1950s and 1960s was a driver's paradise.

It's hard for the family to imagine not having the two classic Porsches, cars that have shaped their lives and memories. Yet the connection nearly missed. At first, Arthur had his eye on another now-classic machine.

Inspired by their fondness for racing, Ruth and Arthur used to work at events in the Bay Area. "We raced first at 17-Mile Drive in Monterey," he says. "They would rope off part of it and movie stars would come and put their tents up inside." But a

Ruth, Arthur, and friends had fun driving Porsches as everyday cars. The white coupe here is not the birthday gift.

fatal accident put an end to it. So the racers went to the Army and got permission to build a track at Laguna Seca. The Shiffrars followed the action and got a job working one corner. The Brittons also worked at the track.

It was the era of the 300SL Gullwing, Mercedes's beautiful, fierce, and unforgiving creation. In manning their post, the Shiffrars were told, "Don't black flag a 300SL because you see the back axles moving around. That's the way they're built."

Their corner's "boss guy" had one and Arthur had told him he wanted to buy it. Finally, the weekend racing day came when the corner boss had a new demeanor. "I have a surprise for you," he said. "My 300SL is for sale for $5,000. I saved it for you."

But he had kept the Shiffrars waiting for a sports car too long. They had come to the races that day in their new Convertible D. "I had a friend with a '56 coupe," Arthur recalls, "and it used to go good. It was a good little car, so I bought one to be like him." That friend was Don Britton, and together they drove their Porsches hard.

Often when the two friends were alone in their cars—without wives and their attendant wisdom—Britton would try to

get away. He was a good driver with a decent chance of success. One night as they returned from a trip up the coast, Britton's 356 darted into the night. Arthur Shiffrar mashed the pedal, but his chum had gotten the jump. So Arthur employed a trick of his own: He doused the lights.

The two Porsches were nearly alone, flat-footing the straights, downshifting and powering through corners, reveling in a moonlit cat-and-mouse on the cliffs above the sea. One car passed the other way—a government-appointed cat-and-mouse catcher. In an instant he had whipped around and gotten into Shiffrar's mirror, red light flashing its unique brand of disapproval.

The officer was on his way home for the evening ready to end his law-enforcement day. Lights-out racing pressed the wrong button. "I would have let you go," he said. "I don't care if you got killed, but I'd hate to see that Porsche go tumbling down some cliff into the ocean." As the patrolman handed Shiffrar a fat ticket, Britton pulled up and parked on the other side of the road. He kept his grin concealed from the officer.

The Shiffrars did not limit their miles in the Convertible D to leisurely or speedy drives along the California coast. "We

Use can eventually destroy a car, but it is also what creates the stories that make it so memorable and precious. While the red car is the same in all of these photos, the low bumper visible here distinguishes this older car from Genevieve's white coupe.

The paint on the coupe is actually a Corvette shade, but it suits the car. It was sprayed some twenty-five years ago and was a quality job. It's the only paint Genevieve has known the car to wear, and the color is tied to all her Porsche-driving memories.

drove the pants off it," Arthur says. One summer, he quit his job. "We circumnavigated the United States, threw our sleeping bags in, and ate cheap on soup and sandwiches." They drove the little Porsche to Yellowstone, up into Canada to Quebec and Niagara Falls, and down the East Coast. A Pontiac rear ended them in New York, but Arthur pulled out the dent by hand and they kept going. They drove for three months, carrying on to Florida, then back through New Orleans, Texas, and New Mexico. "We made it home in time for Ruth to go back to work," Arthur laughs. "Best trip we ever made."

Selling the Convertible D never occurred to the Shiffrars. That would be like selling your arm. Instead, as the miles accrued and daughters arrived, they bought other, bigger vehicles. When Maggie turned sixteen, these car-loving parents passed along the most meaningful thing they could give for her to drive. To make it special for their first child's big birthday, they painted the car—long before the "survivor" concept took hold. The correct red wasn't available, so they chose another shade that suited the car.

Arthur also swapped the engine once to rebuild it, but the original is back in the car. Apart from routine maintenance items, little else has changed.

If giving a sixteen-year-old an extraordinary Porsche convertible seems risky, there's a flip side. "It was a brilliant move," Maggie thinks. "There was nothing I could do in town they couldn't find out about." She drove it to school every day, where the history teacher with the classroom closest to the parking lot was informally charged with keeping an eye on it. This was the same school where their mother and Dorothy Britton taught, so the car was well known.

Instead of messing with it, as one might expect from teen-agers, fellow students admired and respected the car and actually looked out for it too. Somehow a convertible Porsche was beyond the typical pranks students play on each other when the cars don't mean much.

Yet a Porsche can inspire mischief in those around it. One of Maggie's fondest memories in the car parallels her father's. At graduate school one day, in the heart of Stanford's campus, she came to a red light in the long-serving Convertible D. A close friend in a 1970s American sedan pulled up beside her and gunned the engine.

Game on.

Maggie wound up the air-cooled boxer four and popped the clutch at the first flick of green. Her eight-cylinder rival got off more slowly, then powered by, rocketing through the next light and past an incredulous patrolman. He stopped the throttle-happy lead sled and Maggie pulled over nearby, sending the same sort of grin out of the 356 that had mocked its way in by the ocean years before.

In the early years, the Porsches were daily transportation for the Shiffrar sisters, but other vehicles have assumed that role. Today, the 356s sit idle mostly. They could use an oil change and some brake freshening perhaps, but they are emphatically not for sale. Nor is there any plan to strip away or cover up the marks, spots, scratches, and wear that tell the cars' life stories.

To passersby, this is a rare pair of Porsches—a surprising sight that might prompt some to wheel up and ask about buying them. They won't get anywhere. The Shiffrar family has owned these cars for a total of nearly seventy-five years.

G. SHIFFRAR/T. GRUBBA

"Whatever happened in my life, I would never sell that car," says Genevieve. "It's not even a possibility."

Maggie's devotion is just as strong. "When I was in grad school, a guy walked up to me and offered $80,000 for the car. I told him, forget it. . . . It would be sacrilege selling it."

Such cars, beautiful and storied, kept for love of what they are not what they're worth, lie at the heart of the survivor philosophy. They wear their past. They are their past. The 356 coupe and Convertible D are unlike one another and unlike all other cars.

This car belonged to Mark Haines's father in the 1960s. Memories of pulling himself into its back seat and his general love for the car inspired Haines to hunt down a classic 'Bird of his own.

Haines and son Hayden are lifelong car fans. Wife Grace enjoys them, too, and drives a classic Beetle. The Thunderbird is one of their favorite cars to take to events because of its comfort and style.

CHAPTER 12

Mark Haines's 1962
London-Texas Thunderbird

ALL ENTHUSIASTS REMEMBER that first meaningful car: how it smelled, where the shifter was, and how it worked, the location and design of the door handles, and the gauges' arrangement and script. Because most of us rode in the back seat, we remember its shape and upholstery, the backs of the front seats, the look of the headliner, transmission tunnel, and carpet, and the huge-to-a-kid shelf below the rear window.

Mark Haines's most distant memories conjure a stylish black car, low, gothic, and elegant. He remembers climbing into its futuristic interior at age two or three, across red vinyl seats, and marveling at the detail inside. The place was southeastern Pennsylvania. The car, his father's 1961 Ford Thunderbird. In the same recesses where such thoughts are stored, he also knew he would own such a car one day.

Years of vicarious car-magazine living and keenly studying everything on the road put other vehicles in his mind, including Chevrolet's Camaro. He had a pristine '77 Type LT through college—a car his father bought him for earning a full scholarship to Villanova—and only let it go when he took a job in England. The Camaro served him well, but it did not displace that distant vision of the low-slung Thunderbird. In fact, he kept a photo of that car on his shelf in London, one photo from among the hundreds of his past that he seized and framed and kept nearby.

His work as an investment banker brought Haines back to the United States at times, including a trip to Houston, Texas, in 2003. What better place to shop for a car than America's

143

In the land of the Stones and the Beatles, a low black car oozing sexy elegance looks at home, even if it spent most of its life with a woman who drove it while wearing white gloves. Haines wanted a convertible, but this unrestored car was so nice he snapped it up on sight.

immense South, a land free of salt and much of the dampness that feasts on northern steel. For his quarry, he settled on a third-generation T-Bird in black with a red interior.

That instant-gratification machine, the Internet, got his pulse up. A well-known Texas classics dealer had a black-and-red convertible, restored, immaculate. But a quick call doused the fire; the drop-top was sold. Rather than quit the idea, Haines sharpened his focus. There was another 'Bird advertised privately. It was not a gleaming restoration, however. In photos, this Ford looked dusty and neglected. It was black, though, and the seller sounded sincere. She had inherited it from her grandmother, wasn't using it, and had reluctantly decided to sell. They arranged to meet.

Even as it dominated his thoughts, an early 1960s Thunderbird was a car Haines had not seen in the real, full-scale, three-dimensional world in many years. Beatles reunions are as common in London. He and the seller, Audra, set a meeting point any out-of-towner could find: Nasa Drive, right by Houston's space center. On his way, Haines caught

something out of the corner of his eye, a dark shape unlike anything on the road.

"Jesus, that car's cool," he thought. It was the Thunderbird.

While it lacked the red vinyl, this Raven Black coupe with Pearl Beige interior had a certain presence, a sense of authenticity. Haines worked through university in the local Ferrari dealership and looked after several private collections. Now he has his own. He has studied many cars. Beneath its dust in the Houston sun was a vintage T-Bird that had dodged bodger, customizer, and skillful restorer alike. Forty years on, this rolling showcase of Ford style wore its original paint, upholstery, and carpets. Under the hood, the original 390 V-8 sat with factory finish, decals, wiring, and radiator. Audra had been guarding a time capsule, the car her grandmother bought new and drove daily throughout her life, making the trek from her home in North Carolina to see family in Texas.

The clock showed 24,000 miles and for a moment Haines's mind reeled. "It's 124,000," Audra said. "Definitely. This was my grandmother's daily driver."

Behind the wheel, the car gave mixed impressions. It hadn't been driven regularly in a number of years, and the suspension and steering were vague. What hit Haines more was the car's artistry. The 1961 to 1963 Thunderbirds ooze style. Few cars with

By 1962, paints had become more durable. The original black finish on this car has been protected from the sun by garages in the United States and U.K., as has the chrome trim. From more than a few paces, they look perfect.

lines so daring even make a designer's sketchpad. When such eye candy gets to the tangible world it is usually as a concept car and nothing more. But the space age T-Bird penned for 1961 cleared all hurdles to emerge from Ford's production line with its arresting futurism intact.

Tending the thin wheel, looking over that broad, black hood, Haines quipped, "It's such an elegant car, I feel like I should be wearing white gloves." Audra's jaw dropped and she looked at him sideways. "My grandmother always wore white gloves to drive this car," she said. (The glove box in the T-bird, by the way, is as unusual as the rest of the car, resting between the seats rather than on the dashboard as most other Detroit products do it.)

Their meeting had the feel of destiny. Haines told her he had always wanted a Thunderbird because it was the first car he could remember. Audra said that that was the reason she owned this one. From the time she was a little girl, she had loved the car and would sit on her grandmother's lap, driving the Thunderbird around the garden. When the grandmother passed away, she left the car to the girl she knew would treasure it as she had.

Yet honored as she was to get it, Audra had found no good use for the car. She garaged it, started it up, and took it for periodic short drives to keep everything working. But it was a classic car. She couldn't see making it her daily driver, and she wasn't involved with any other enthusiasts or clubs that gave the T-Bird more meaning. She hadn't registered the car in Texas, nor secured an insurance policy reflective of the car's collector value. Audra was cautious to drive it more than a short way for fear someone might hit her. Even in her hands, the old black Ford still felt like her grandmother's car.

She decided to let the T-Bird go, though she was worried over what would become of it. She didn't want it to become

The artistic interior shows almost no wear; only the dash pad and the tops of the doors suffered heavily from years of unrelenting southern U.S. sun. Replacing them was not so hard a decision. Haines worked with his U.K. mechanic to fit new pads, then find an appropriate color blend to match them with the 1962-vintage upholstery.

MARK HAINES'S 1962 LONDON-TEXAS THUNDERBIRD . 147

"After-burner" taillights have a space-age feel in the third-generation Thunderbird. Temperature extremes can leave lenses faded and crazed, but these original pieces look and function virtually as new.

a low rider, popular for classics in Texas, or to undergo other modifications that would make it a different car from the one her grandmother prized. Haines was an ideal buyer. The car's originality was one of the first things he commented on. He told her he would take it back to England where such cars were rare. Audra thought her grandmother would be happy at this new life for her Thunderbird.

Closing the deal was simple enough. Now the car had to travel a few thousand miles and cross the Atlantic. A little searching led Haines to Jack Barnes, a Thunderbird specialist in Texas. He asked Barnes to handle the whole operation, from making the car more roadworthy to transporting it to the East Coast and getting it shipped to Britain. You can do this "RORO," or roll-on, roll-off, but Haines opted not to take a risk and decided to put the car in its own container.

The car needed work and finding a second T-Bird specialist on the other side of the ocean was unlikely. He had Barnes look at the suspension and also perform one task that undid a bit of originality. The southern sun and forty years of exposure to the environment had punished the car's original dash pad. It was cracked in many places, its internal fibers showing through.

Haines had a hard time convincing himself to pull this original piece out but concluded that its tattiness—right where a person looks constantly at the wheel—was detracting from the rest of the car's charm. Barnes said replacing it required taking apart the whole dash, a costly and time-consuming venture, yet one Haines wanted the specialist to perform. With suspension and steering fixed and a new dash pad, the '62 Thunderbird traveled to the East Coast, boarded a ship, and arrived in England.

Early in the car's life, the original owner fitted air conditioning, which was directed into the rear-seat area by ducts beneath the back window. The literature for the unit was included with the car.

Given schedules and geography, Haines didn't meet Barnes; he simply wired him the money for everything. When they spoke during the work, Barnes praised the car. "You have something really special here," he said. "It's been ten or twenty years since I've seen anything like this. Completely original. No one has messed with it."

Back in England Haines's mechanic there reinforced this impression. Following shipment, the car needed to pass its "MoT," England's vehicle inspection named for the Ministry of Transport. Haines had picked up a '62 factory manual, which the British garage referred to in prepping the car for inspection. "This car is completely original," the mechanic said. "If the manual says a blue wire attaches to a red wire, that's exactly

Batteries never last, so this is a modern replacement, but the original washer fluid reservoir is tougher than it looks. Maybe there's something to the perfectly legible slogan across the bottom: "made right . . . fit right . . . last longer."

what we found." Very few cars stay that way over the decades, he remarked, because wires get cut, added, and replaced during repairs, modifications, and upgrades.

One exhaust manifold was cracked, which Haines replaced with a U.S.-wrecking-yard item at his mechanic's suggestion because it would be heat seasoned and original. When they swapped that out, the mechanic observed that no one had torn into the engine. All the original locking nuts are still in place.

The replacement dash pad comes in black, a situation Haines corrected in the U.K. He and the shop found an unfaded area by the doors that represented the original Pearl Mist shade. To get it all to blend right, they custom dyed the pad and the tops of the door upholstery. The important thing is that the result looks natural, suiting this unrestored classic's age and condition.

With the suspension fixed and a full alignment, the car negotiated England's winding roads like a far newer vehicle. A few bugs had to be worked out, however. On one of the car's first trips, to the south coast town of Worthing for a classic car show called Sunny Sunday—which wasn't—years of non-use made a loud statement. One of the front brakes had stuck and seized from rust, while the 390 V-8 continued to push the car onward. When they finally got out in a muddy parking lot, Haines and his

family got only a few strides before a loud Bang, Hiss, erupted behind them. The tire by the stuck brake blew from the heat and the radiator sprung a leak on cue when the front of the car dropped toward the mud. It was a screwball-comedy moment that a few folks nearby applauded. They also rushed to help, however, and got the tire changed out. A local garage repaired the radiator.

When the T-Bird had its fiftieth anniversary in 2005, England's Thunderbird club had a large gathering. Haines took his car and learned that a contingent of fellow Americans had come over for the show. Asking if any of them knew Jack Barnes, Haines learned that the man who got his car to England was there at the show. When they met for the first time face-to-face, Barnes gave Haines a hug—a gesture those who know him said was unheard of.

"People like you are insane," Barnes said. "You send me all this money and you don't even know me. I could have done anything with that money." Talk soon turned to the car and the

The mufflers are unlikely to be the very ones fitted in 1962, but they have the correct look. One of the few things that needed replacing on the car was one exhaust manifold. On his mechanic's advice, Haines installed a period, seasoned one from a U.S. wrecking yard, rather than a modern replacement.

SIMON BURTWELL

There may be a hose or two replaced here, and the engine immobilizer key by the radiator is recent, but virtually everything else is untouched '62 Ford. When you've left the outside unrestored, this is the look you want underhood.

1962 Ford Thunderbird

Condition	A survivor: an original, unrestored car. Paint, interior, and engine are all original (only the dashpad & seatbelts have been renewed)
Colour & Trim	Raven Black with "Pearl Beige" interior
Model Year	Thunderbirds were completely restyled every 3 years. The 61 – 63 cars are often known as "bullet birds", with side trim and front grill differing between those years
Options	Air-conditioning (dealer installed 1966) Tinted glass Fender skirts Pushbutton radio Seatbelts Side mirror
History	Bought new in May 1962 by Audie Mae Byrd Camp of Old Fort North Carolina. Inherited by her granddaughter in 1998 from whom the car was purchased in 2003. The purchase included the original documentation, etched highball glasses and scale model which came with the car when new
Drivetrain	390 c.i. (6.4L) 300 hp V-8, 4 bbl carb, dual exhaust, automatic transmission

fun Barnes's employee had cleaning it up. He found coins from the 1960s that were still like new under the carpets.

His grandmother-owned 1962 Ford Thunderbird is special to Haines for more than its originality. He likes the thought that his son, like him, will count crawling into the back seat of this car among his earliest memories. I met father and son in England several years ago and had a good look at the Thunderbird from Texas, now proudly wearing its U.K. registration plates. I sat down behind the wheel and son, Hayden, two years old, stood on the passenger seat. Taking in that wild and stylish interior, he looked over his surroundings with genuine appreciation, then said in a little boy's British accent, "It's pretty nice, isn't it?"

Yes, it is.

Use 'em if you got 'em.
There are defensible
trailer queens: cars so
ancient and important to
automotive history that the
risk of breakage is more
significant than the glacial
movement they provide.
Leaving a Cobra sit is like
raising Walter Payton and
prohibiting him from playing
sports. It's just wrong.

CHAPTER 13

The Portland Barris 427/428 Shelby Cobra

IN THE 1960S AND 1970S, taking the wheel of a Cobra ranked right up there in young men's minds with dating Ann-Margret or Jacqueline Bisset—and was hardly more likely. A teenager getting hold of Shelby's voracious hybrid was remote fantasy, the sort of far-flung vision that gets restless minds through a dry lecture on the first day of spring.

Jim Maxwell had it better. If some young men work overtime to avoid the burden of a younger sibling, Maxwell's older brother, Ed, did him the ultimate favor. He bought an AC Shelby 289 Cobra, an audacious move for someone just out of medical school. So audacious, in fact, he had to borrow money from Jim, a high school senior, to make it happen. As sure as the Shelby feasted on slower road-traveling animals, the terms of that loan included seat time at the throttle. (There were other controls, too, but what were they, again?)

The Maxwell brothers—there are three—first ran Corvairs. They had five or six over the years, which they wrenched on and ran in gymkhanas and solo events. The Cobra was new territory, a Phantom F4-J when you're used to flying Cessnas. Because Ed was doing a medical internship, Jim got to drive the 289 roadster "all the time."

After Ed blew up the engine, putting the car back on the road was going to cost $500. Today, keeping a Cobra alive for that price is a laugh—we pay that for a Honda brake job—but in 1972, it was money to think twice about. With other concerns and demands to occupy him, Ed sold the car. Seeing it go

Those in the Cobra camp often refer to their low-production sports cars by manufacturer's ID number. It's what separates the look-alikes from the genuine machines.

suddenly brought home how special Jim Maxwell's life had been with ready access to such an extraordinary road craft.

He knew he would have another Cobra, but career aspirations pushed that point into the uncertain future. He had plans to become a physician himself, a goal that would absorb his energies and resources for years to come. During his residency, he bought a '67 Corvette to fill the sports car void. Nice car though it was, it proved an imperfect stand-in for the true object of his devotion.

By 1987, his miles in a Shelby had been memories long enough. He found a seller with a 289 version. The original engine came with the car but was no longer in it. The seller had three of the smaller-engine Cobras and swapped motors and other parts around as needed to keep the one or two he drove regularly running. He blew the engine in one of those cars and had swapped in the V-8 from the car he was now selling. When he fixed the blown motor, he put that one in the sale car because he really didn't mind which engine was in which car. Maxwell, of course, did care; he left a down payment on a promise that the seller would reinstall the factory-fitted Ford mill and be in

touch. As the date on his deposit check slid into the past, Maxwell began to doubt whether the man would come through. When he saw another Cobra offered by a dealer, he bought it.

The first seller was no deadbeat, though—far from it. He finished the car and called Maxwell, standing on their original offer even though 289 values had climbed $30,000 in the interim. Suddenly Maxwell had what he wanted twofold. Both of his road-rockets were powered by the small-block engine he preferred. Special cars don't come available according to our wants and needs, however, and car lovers are ever searching, even when the garage is full or the wallet empty.

A 427 car had never captivated him. Maxwell's first glorious experience, as a Shelby-powered teenager, was with a 289. That car so outperformed everything else he'd driven that the need for more cubic inches and power did not arise. It wasn't displacement that seized him when his eyes met a Cobra ad in *Hemmings Motor News* in 2000. The magic lay in the car's condition: unrestored, with its original paint. So long have Cobras been currency in the collector car scene, most of them have been restored at least once if not several times. A car appointed just

The top is functional, if hard to raise, but Maxwell seldom uses it. If he's in motion when rain starts, he just stays on the pedal. Most drops clear the passenger compartment at speed. The license plate is funny yet unnecessary. It's the owners of totally restored cars who most often get that irksome inquiry, "Is it real?"

Original owner, Pino, used a key-operated alarm when he was at sea. Maxwell's about driving the car, not messing with it. Pino's switch will stay in place, another historic marker.

as the original owner had had it more than thirty years before was irresistible.

Maxwell called the seller, who was buying a home in Boca Raton, Florida, and offering the Cobra to free up a few greenbacks. They struck a deal for less than the asking price. The following day, several other aspiring owners called with higher offers, but once again Maxwell had a seller who stuck by his word.

The big-block Cobra is unusual in several ways. Most noticeable is the paint. "The paint is terrible," Maxwell laughs. "Ten feet away in the sunlight it shines, but up close it looks like a dried-up riverbed." So he'll soon be respraying it, right? Not in this life. "Terrible" is an adjective requiring context—an objective judgment compared to fresh paint's smooth shine. Personally, Maxwell loves the fractured finish; it's what gives the car character. And it's no ordinary coat of its day.

The pearl white paint on Maxwell's 427 was applied when the car was new at a cost of $2,000. The second owner saw the car sitting on the showroom floor at Marv Tonkin Ford in Portland, Oregon, in 1967, but he lacked the means to buy it at the time. Another man bought it, a merchant seaman from Portland named Al Pino—at least that's how the name sounds. Maxwell

There is enough mother-of-pearl shine to fool the eye from a distance. Up close, the paint looks, in Maxwell's words, like a dried-up riverbed. This riverbed, however, is on the Maxwell Originality Registry and won't be removed or covered up.

has tried to track him down using that spelling and others with no luck.

In this case, the pearl finish contains the material for which it is named, mother of pearl, hand-ground and blended into the paint. The gold dust that accompanies it is likewise the real thing. These features contributed to the paint job's price, but so did the customization guru behind it—George Barris. Maxwell has a copy of the car's original invoice from Shelby American, which shipped the car to Portland on February 15, 1967. The invoice indicates the color as silver, which is how the car left England. Tonkin ordered the Barris Kustom paint job, which the car apparently received before it left Los Angeles. In spring 2008, Maxwell was fortunate enough to meet Barris at a car show on the East Coast and to show him the Cobra. Barris told him that he recognized the car and remembered the paint job, confirming the way in which he created the pearl content.

From its early days, the car had a burglar alarm, fitted by or for Pino, as well as a hardtop and Plexiglas windows. Pino would hot rod around Portland on shore leave, then set up the top and windows, activate the alarm, and park the car while at sea. He operated the anti-theft system with a key switch placed

Not the slickest politician or the best poker player could get away with saying he had no interest in taking the controls of this beast. That would be like a drooling lion telling a zebra, "Sit down, relax, I just want to talk—don't worry, I already ate."

in front of the 427 badge on the driver's side. Like the paint, this switch remains undisturbed.

Another unusual feature on this car, chassis number CSX 3288—the way Cobra owners refer to them—is the engine. Though branded and sold as a 427, that is not the exact displacement underhood. Despite Shelby's deal with Ford, he was competing with NASCAR teams for the potent 427 side-oiler V-8. It was also expensive, more than twice the cost of its big-block sibling, the 428. When fitting side-oilers grew more difficult, Maxwell says, Shelby made a quiet swap. According to the Shelby Registry, about one hundred cars labeled and sold as 427s actually bore the 428 Police Interceptor engine, which saved Shelby hundreds of dollars per build, though he kept the price the same. Buyers discovered the discrepancy and complained, as a result of which almost all of the cars that left Shelby American with an extra cubic inch have been retrofitted with 427s. Maxwell says the number of intact 428s now stands at about eleven.

Even if you've never seen a 427 Cobra in three dimensions, odds are decent you've watched Michael Sarrazin at the wheel of one in *The Gumball Rally*. Footage of the reverse-wind speedometer's needle turned well past the 100 mark appears often.

As with the paint, anyone anticipating Maxwell to jump on this engine issue and change things around will have a long, long wait. The retrofitted cars can be justified because they are now the way they were supposed to be. But CSX 3288's engine bay has the 428 Shelby put there. That's all Maxwell needs to know. Besides, the Cobra is hardly sluggish propelled by a Police Interceptor's 360 horses and torque boatload. He drives this car on public roads often and never wants for more push. Precious few vehicles can put his headlights in their rearview mirror if Maxwell doesn't want them to.

A prior owner puts the car's oomph in perspective. He had his banker, the man who ponied up the dough, driving the car on an airport access road. The owner invited his lender to give it some pedal. The uninitiated banker floor-boarded the throttle, snapping the tires free instantaneously and pitching the front end off the direction of travel. At some 50 degrees of rotation the shell-shocked banker finally unglued his go-foot, allowing the roaring Shelby's nose to come back in front of the rear wheels. The owner nearly had a heart-attack and he can only assume the banker felt no better. Cobra history makes clear that it's unwise to stand on the throttle until you fully appreciate what's about to happen. Having heard "this car is fast" is woefully insufficient warning.

Maxwell is the car's seventh owner, making survival of the original paint and interior all the more impressive. As far as Maxwell knows, CSX 3288 also has its original carpets, seats, rubber mats, plug wires, hose clamps, and most everything else.

Non-original items are few. The air cleaner and exhaust system have been replaced. Although Maxwell thinks the Sunburst wheels are the original style, someone may have fitted wider ones at the back, as a prior owner recalls them being equal width front and rear. At some point, the front suspension A-arms and ball joints were upgraded. The tool kit is there, but missing the screwdriver—an item Maxwell will go to great lengths to replace with an original piece. While the seats are original, he wonders whether someone may have had them restuffed. If not, they've held up surprisingly well, but then again mileage is low.

The car's records also chart rising Cobra values. The invoice from Shelby American shows a price of $6,294.63, including $149 for freight. Another document, which Maxwell doesn't actually have in hand, lists the $2,000 for the Barris paint job, making the total cost for the car more than $8,000 when first sold. The second owner paid $12,000 in 1973. In 1977 or 1978, the third owner bought it for $19,000, then sold it four years later for $48,000. The buyer at that price may have been a

dealer, who turned around and resold it the same year, 1982, for $65,000. The sixth owner got CSX 3288 plus other cars and cash for a genuine Ford GT 40. Maxwell paid $225,000 for the 427/428 Cobra in May 2000.

While some in the ownership chain acquired the car as an investment, Maxwell bought it for what it is, an unrestored example of Carroll Shelby's legend. He got it to drive and does so whenever the temperature is above 50 degrees in North Carolina. Mainly he likes back-road adventures, but he's had some unaggressive track time too. Owner six drove it only a few hundred miles and stored it about ten years. Prior owners had put a little more than 21,000 miles on it, to which he's already added 6,000.

His car does not have the roll bar and side pipes many people associate with the 427 Cobra. Only a small number were outfitted that way, he notes. A toy manufacturer came out and took photos and measurements of his car, so perhaps that

Carpets reveal where drivers since the late 1960s have placed and moved their feet. Pedal lettering is evocative of the era when AC and Shelby built this two-seat symbol of speed and style.

Maxwell was fortunate enough to meet George Barris at a car event. He told the customizing legend that word was he'd painted Maxwell's Cobra. Barris recognized it immediately and explained how he'd made the paint. He signed the inside of the glove box door to authenticate his handiwork.

perception will shift if children begin to play with toy big-block Cobras like this one.

Although the car has already changed hands six times, Maxwell has considered selling CSX 3288 only once, when both of his sons were hammering him with Duke University tuition expenses. That would have been a cruel twist, given which of his three children truly loves this car. When he acquired this Shelby after ten years of storage, Maxwell needed to rebuild a few things, including the brakes. After a long day's work, when he lay underneath the Cobra, wrench in hand, he often heard footsteps, followed by the other creeper making its way across the garage floor. His eager helper was daughter, Leigh, then twelve years old.

She helped him bleed the brakes and studied other systems Maxwell checked and worked on. Her affinity for the car has continued to grow. She is often at the wheel when he is not, and parting with this Cobra is no longer an option.

"That's my car, Dad," Leigh has told him. "You can't sell it, and I get it when you're gone." Forget your offers, fellow survivor fans. The lady has spoken.

If you knew nothing about what car terms go with what eras, you still might match this photo and the concept "muscle car." This unrestored Hemi go-mobile looks like a world class sprinter crouched in the blocks. The Lime Green Superbird in the garage beyond has been repainted (its original color) but is otherwise unrestored. Yes, it's a Hemi four-speed car.

Mo'par to Ya:
Greg Nelsen's Hemi Treats

FEW OF US WHO SIZED UP A ROAD RUNNER, Challenger, Charger, or 'Cuda as something we'd like to lay some rubber in back in high school would have imagined that these budget-built torquemobiles would surpass in value the homes we were raised in. Greg Nelsen got the message early.

The same flashy colors, predatory lines, and chest-thumping exhaust notes that keep auction paddles waving called to Nelsen when Chrysler first started offering these audacious cars to rebellious young men. Yet a new one was just beyond reach. It wasn't until a nasty car accident reminded him how short life can be that Nelsen decided he had done without a Mopar muscle car long enough.

He tracked down a suitable candidate in Wisconsin and dragged his patient wife along for a look. It was a '70 Charger with 440 six-pack (three two-barrel carburetors) V-8 and a Hurst pistol-grip shifter stout enough for train-yard work but fitted to the car's four-speed transmission. Nelsen gave it the inspector-detective treatment inside and out and then convinced the seller to let him drive it back to Minnesota so a dealership mechanic,

This Curious Yellow Hemi 'Cuda was bought new by John and Esther George of California. They drove it until the car became such a hot collectible, idiots would try to take parts off of it if they parked it in public.

Finally, John George decided to anchor the car to the garage floor. When Greg Nelsen bought the car, he took the anchor too—part of this unrestored rarity's interesting history.

his friend Dan Nord, could throw it on a lift for even closer scrutiny. The car passed all tests.

Finally Nelsen could look out over his own Mopar hood from the driver's seat. Briefly.

It wasn't an accident or the men and women in blue that took the Charger away. It was his friends! They didn't want a ride. They didn't want a drive. They wanted the car, and they were very persistent. Nelsen had scraped together six grand for the big-block Dodge and he barely warmed up the seat before a friend offered him ten.

Well, shoot. Yeah, he wanted the car but how many investments can you make 70 percent on almost overnight?

Nelsen traded the keys for the coin and bought another Mopar. The same thing happened. Instead of whistles and nods—maybe the occasional stoplight challenge from a Camaro or Chevelle—every spin he took in the car brought more former high school dreamers out of hiding with their checkbooks. No matter how hard he tried to treat his Mopar as a car, other people saw it as treasure.

Where did he get it?

What does he want for it?

Nelsen, right, hires his friend, Dan Nord, to keep his various cars in good running condition. That's fine with Nord, who is also a tried-and-true Mopar fan and owner. Nord checked out Nelsen's first Mopar purchase way back when.

TOM WITTA

Can he find another one?

Please, they seemed to say, "*Get me what you got.*"

Regardless what he paid the guy on his right, there was always someone on his left with a bigger bag of money. It was like one day everyone agreed that leaves were an ideal currency and the only one around with a rake was Nelsen.

Mopar speculating reached far and wide, giving every hulk and part some cash value from decent to indecent. Sure you can get burned in this market and any other, but Nelsen was not a born hustler. He was a born Mopar fan, and he learned whatever he could about the cars he loved. Much of the learning was details—what went with what, how to read a VIN, where to find a build sheet. But another part, the one that separates the aimless hunter from the guy who bags the big game, was learning how to find and buy cars. Mostly he buys them because he loves them. Yet there's always another buyer who wants his Mopars even more, enough to pay an irresistible sum. And Nelsen has to move a few cars to fund the thrill of bringing new finds home.

As with other collector niches, it's the original cars, with the paint and the goodies the manufacturer first gave them, that Moparphiles get most hot and bothered about. While Nelsen has

With values gone crazy, there's a lot of Mopars like the one on the right that once looked like those on the left. In this case, the Gunmetal Grey Challenger is unrestored with its original paint.

For some reason, the prior owner had fitted wide mirrors. Was he planning to tow with his Hemi Challenger? Nelsen had no use for those mirrors but did not want to respray a car with an otherwise excellent and rare-color paint. Instead, he filled and spot painted just the holes, but not the surrounding area, to minimize changes to the finish.

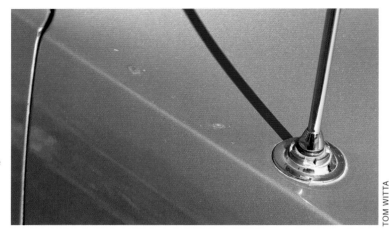

many tales of hunting Dodge and Plymouth in the wild, two cars stand out among his favorite trophies—a '71 Hemi 'Cuda bought from the original owner out of a garage so small the passenger had to get out before the car went in, and a '71 Gunmetal Grey Hemi Challenger.

The 'Cuda he named "Curious George" because the paint was Curious Yellow and he bought it from the original California owner, John George. Nelsen heard about the car through the grapevine. He knew a guy who knew a guy who knew about the car. That's how it often starts. Nelsen said he wanted the number, but it's seldom that easy. He bought some original Mopar wheels and tires off the California contact for a handsome price, and that got him the phone listing.

Many calls earned the owner's trust, but just enough to meet Nelsen—and not at the owner's home. By then seventy years old, the 'Cuda's title holder had driven the car until people started paying too much attention to it. When somebody tried to steal the shaker hood off of it while it was parked in public, George put it away. He put it away and he locked it with a ship chain to a ship anchor. If anybody did pull off stealing the thing, it would be a job for the movies.

Nelsen wasn't close to taking that chain off the front. For now, he and the owner were out at Pannekoeken having a nice time. But talking about selling and watching the car you bought new drive off with somebody else's mitts on the wheel are two different things. George liked Nelsen, was impressed with his knowledge of cars, and enjoyed trading stories. He wasn't ready to sell, though, not even when Nelsen showed him that he had brought cash—real cash; not a check, not a money order, not a note from his banker—real paper money with a three-digit symbol like this in each corner: 100. George was more impressed. Impressed and still not selling.

For two years Nelsen stayed in touch. There was a big Mopar show on the Left Coast, which provided a fine opportunity to get back out there and talk to Mr. George some more. "I don't live next door to this guy," Nelsen said. If he was going to get that car, he felt like he needed to close a deal on this trip.

He called his old friend and they went back and forth on where to meet this time. Finally George invited Greg to meet him at the house. When you don't plan to sell something and you invite over a guy hell bent on buying it, maybe your heart has some news for your head: You *are* willing to sell it. Possibly. At the very least you're willing to talk some more. There's a lot of women in the world who sit down to breakfast each morning across from a man they declined more than once when the phone rang. Yet there they sit.

Nelsen never misled George or his wife, Esther. When they went to the garage for a look—Nelsen hadn't even seen the car when he made an offer on his first trip—he set a meaningful pile of cash on the hood. "I'm not leaving till I get this car," he said. The sight of the money made John uneasy. "We're starving," he said. "Let's go get breakfast."

They had a nice meal—hardcore Mopar fans jawing about their favorite cars—then went back to the house. When he went in the bathroom, Nelsen left ten thousand dollars in cash spread out on the vanity. Then the kitchen. Everywhere he went in the house, he laid out a pile of cash and each one brought a new exclamation from the Georges. They lived in a little house from the 1960s with carpet worn down to the backing. A fast car chained

TOM WITTA

to an anchor in the garage wasn't making their lives much better, not even an all original '71 Hemi 'Cuda four-speed.

"John, you know it's time," Nelsen said. "You've had the fun, the memories, the history. Take the money and treat yourself and Esther." By this point, piles of 100s were cluttering the house. Finally John asked how much money was there. When Nelsen told him, George responded, "You're hard on an old guy." He didn't hand over the keys, though.

They went around some more, laughing and joking the whole time. "What are we supposed to do with all this money?" Esther said. "Take off your clothes and roll in it," Nelsen offered. "It's all cool and crisp." Esther laughed hard. "I'll stick around for that show," John said, not gathering the keys or title.

"Let's have a beer," John said. Nelsen reached into his pocket and pulled out a cashier's check for another ten thousand. He'd taken all the local branch's cash that morning. He put the check on the pile. "How much more do I gotta bleed?" he asked.

The answer was a little more. George loved that car and he knew it was valuable. He and Esther had had a lot of memories with it. They'd squeaked past it in their little garage for decades, grazing their butts off one fender. The constant contact rubbed the paint off but George was an experienced painter. He'd touched it up and done quite a nice job, Nelsen says. That little bit of paintwork was the only thing on the car that wasn't

TOM WITTA

bone stock. Even the original plug wires still snaked from the distributor to the distinctive Hemi heads.

It had been morning when Mopar-man came calling and now the Pacific was cutting off the sun's last rays. Nelsen and the Georges had laughed and talked and eaten, had some beer, and laughed a lot more. The interview, the audition, the test of character, honesty, integrity, and humanity that characterizes the transfer of a prized possession to a new generation had come to a close.

John's voice was soft now, solemn for the first time. "She's yours," he said. "You want her more than I do." Nelsen wanted to collapse, but John had a better idea—showing him his old fishing tackle from the 1920s. "I don't know if I can find the title," Esther said. "Then I guess I'll be living here," Nelsen threw back as they headed for the garage.

When John and Nelsen got back from checking out the fishing gear, Esther had found the title. And the window sticker. And every piece of paper the Georges had ever received on the car. They closed the deal and Nelsen flew back to Minnesota.

Interior is likewise unrestored. Yes, it's a four-speed car. Most of a Challenger's interior is plastic; this one is not cracked, warped, or faded.

Up close there are a few paint blemishes visible. They are minor, symptoms of a driven car. Repainting something this original would almost surely harm rather than help value.

TOM WITTA

Word on the all original '71 Hemi 'Cuda four-speed moved faster than sound through cables, satellites, and relay towers. Friends and acquaintances hammered on Nelsen from day one, offering him 50 percent over his purchase price before the car arrived in his home state. Nelsen was stunned. "Now I knew how John felt," he said.

He resisted for several years, savoring the best find of his Mopar career. But his heart was talking to his head, passing along offers from a collector down South. It was a man Nelsen knew and trusted, who had taken several of his cars before. He had every intention of taking this one and no plan for backing off.

The offer was getting big. The tipping point was at hand.

When the money wrench twisted his arm to the breaking point, Nelsen gave in. But he didn't want a semi trailer heaped with bills; he wanted more cars. *Curious George* went for another '71 Hemi Cuda, a '70 Hemi Cuda plus a '71 Hemi convertible 'Cuda clone. Whew.

The other original Mopar Nelsen most cherishes is a Gunmetal Grey four-speed Hemi Challenger, one of seventy built. Nelsen started chasing it in the 1980s, but the owner held fast. He had pulled the motor and was planning to make some heavy-hitter drag car. Yanking the stock mill was as far as he got.

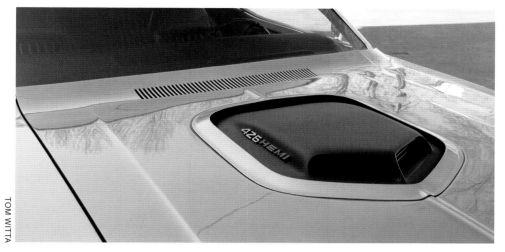

Everyone knows the collector magic in the word (or half word) "Hemi." Dash and seats have not been touched. Those are the exact pieces that came from Dodge in '71.

Original floor mats are hard to come by because of the dirt and abrasive action they confront with every ride. This car saw little use, so even the floors are nice.

The car sat in a heated garage surrounded by the owner's many toolboxes for years. Nelsen kept calling and while the owner became a friend, he was not giving up that Challenger.

Sadly, with one of his calls, Nelsen received the tragic news that the owner had died of cancer. The widow had no use for the Challenger and was glad when "the guy from Minnesota" called. She knew the car was a collector vehicle and worth more than the $20,000 other family members were offering. The owner had a son and he really wanted that car, but with the father's passing, the mother felt it was time to sell. Nelsen went out of his way to be nice to the son. He knew what it was like to be young and dreaming of a hot Mopar to call one's own.

Nelsen took his offer to the family in a form all sellers understand, his old standby cash. Not a check or a promise or a certificate—genuine paper you can snap and stack and buy anything in the world with that's for sale. It was a lot more than the relatives were offering. From prior discussions with her husband, the widow had an idea of the Challenger's value. She said Nelsen's offer was enough and the deal was done.

Lucky for Nelsen, even though the owner hadn't completed his engine swap, his approach was orderly. All of the removed parts stayed close to the car and Nelsen gathered up everything. With help from long-term friend Troy Martinson, he was able to reassemble this survivor completely with the original parts. Even years of sitting immobile around tools in a wrench-turner's garage brought no meaningful harm. The paint and metal survived with nary a bruise.

Along with other documents, the family found three titles for it, plus the window sticker. The only thing missing was the build sheet, yet Nelsen had plenty to prove the car's provenance.

His persistence had paid off and so did his good fortune, one more time. After selling the car, the family had an estate sale. Some car guys Nelsen knew went and picked up a few factory service manuals. Tucked inside one of them was a build sheet for a 1971 Gunmetal Grey Dodge Hemi Challenger. Nelsen gave the finder a reward and now has everything to document this extremely original rare-color car. Everything is numbers matching and nothing has been redone.

Even though he bought it in the 1990s, this is a car Nelsen still owns—but people are working on him. He's already turned down a figure with an 8 at the front of it and a lot of zeroes afterward. So far his will is strong. He can't let every precious Mopar he finds go to someone else . . . too easily.

The '72 365 GTB/4
that Stan Reeg bought
recently from the original
owner has excellent
documentation and a fun
history, including trips
through Europe. Reeg
is having the exterior
painted because the
finish was so cracked,
but he's leaving the
interior the Ferrari
factory installed.

CHAPTER 15

Good Medicine: Doc Frost's Ferrari 365GTB/4 Daytona

We all know Jack Frost from our early years of television and children's literature. Around St. Donatus, Iowa, this name means more than winter personified. Dr. John Frost was a bigger deal than his symbolic namesake, a figure larger than life the locals might say.

One fan of the Doc's is Stan Reeg, and for one simple reason. In Reeg's impressionable years, Doc Frost was synonymous with the fastest, sexiest, most desirable cars that tools, design-daring, and race-minded builders ever consolidated into snarling engines and swooping coachwork. The first time Reeg got his nose around the corner of Doc's garage door, he saw five Ferraris, five Corvettes, and three Rolls-Royces.

Those Ferraris—freeze frames of cars happiest dicing up the twisties at 100-plus—burned an image of automotive perfection into Reeg's young mind. If some boys go to bed dreaming of diving catches or center-field rips, Reeg saw a river of pavement disappearing beneath a twelve-cylinder Ferrari's voracious maw. From his first glimpse into that charmed auto stable, Reeg wanted to buy one of Doc's steeds.

In addition to his work as a dermatologist, Doc Frost also ran a speed shop and regularly traveled to Europe to drive or buy fast machinery. While he bought his Ferraris from Bill Harrah— yes, *that* Harrah—Doc was no stranger to the factory in Modena. He traveled there in spring 1973 to pick up this '72 365GTB/4 coupe. He had taken delivery of a prior Daytona in 1972, but just two days after it arrived in the United States, a drunken driver hit the car and destroyed it. Doc promptly ordered another one

It took a number of years, but Stan Reeg finally fulfilled his dream of buying a Ferrari Daytona coupe from his neighbor and hero, Dr. Jack Frost. Frost picked up this car himself, in Italy, and drove the car fast in Europe. He knew and loved fine sports cars.

and arranged to pick it up in Italy. That was a lot more fun and the start of many trips.

On his first visit, he was honored by a meeting with Numero Uno himself, Enzo Ferrari. Because Doc had come to the factory to collect the car, Mr. Ferrari made sure it was up to spec before sending it off. Good thing for the Doc, too, for according to his trip journal, Ferrari discovered that the passenger side vent window whistled at 250 kilometers per hour. Imagine that! Most passenger cars would make far worse noises trying to reach 155 miles per hour—and failing—but this was high-speed art under the man's own nameplate. Ferrari asked master craftsman, Sergio Scaglietti, once owner of the carrozzeria just across the street, if he could rectify the problem; when a window adjustment didn't solve it, Scaglietti replaced the door.

Numero Uno knew his buyers as well as his cars, which is likely why he insisted the vent window be silent at speed. Leaving the factory, Doc did some testing of his own, covering 402 miles to Geneva, Switzerland, in three hours and fifty-two minutes—whistle free. Personalized treatment from Enzo Ferrari and Sergio Scaglietti made this 365 GTB/4 even more special to Doc. (Doc was careful to use only the numeric name for his coupe in Modena. Doc says Mr. Ferrari never referred to

his race-bred twelve-cylinder sports car as a Florida beach, nor did anyone at the factory in his presence.)

Enjoying these super cars on their native soil was so rewarding for the Doc that he took the car back to Europe in 1981 aboard the *QE2* (*Queen Elizabeth II* luxury liner). He and his wife covered more than 5,000 Daytona miles on that trip, visiting Ferrari facilities and events. Doc returned in 1983 and 1985 for similar low-slung sightseeing.

While the Doc tended his horsepower and patients, Reeg built a career of his own. His first prancing horse badge came affixed to a 328, which he bought in 1998. A 550 followed. They also were coupes, the body style Reeg favors for its predominant use in Europe, where Ferrari built its racing reputation. Convertibles, Reeg says, were made for the American market. While his newer models were rewarding to drive, they could not displace Reeg's favorite Ferraris—the ones in his neighbor's garage.

In a town of 150 or so, most people know one another and Doc was well acquainted with his collection's biggest admirer. He had talked to Reeg and his friends since they were wide-eyed

Flash back to 1973. Here is the doctor and his wife, Luella, with Stan's car in Grenoble, France. The Frosts enjoyed fine things, particularly if they were built by Enzo Ferrari. If Luella looks sleepy here, chalk it up to long, fast miles. They had some wonderful experiences in beautiful cars and places.

The Ferrari 365 GTB/4 bears production number 16213. It isn't the first Daytona coupe Frost purchased around 1972. A prior one got hit and destroyed by a drunken driver shortly after delivery to the United States. Second time round, Frost decided to pick up and bring the car back himself.

kids gawking at the Doc's unique and noisy imports. Knowing a man and selling him a special car, however, are two different things. There must be trust. More people admire the world's great automobiles than there are cars to satisfy demand. Owners are guardians, trustees of machines that define driving's pleasures. It takes more than a check crowded with zeroes to earn a set of keys.

Reeg is a patient hunter. A few years had sneaked past from the time he first saw the Doc's Ferraris until the time he had the means to buy one. As the Doc started to slow down, Reeg breached the subject of buying one of his Daytonas—the coupe, of course. He knew the answer would not immediately be yes. This was the start of a process.

Over the months that followed, Reeg continued to talk to Doc, to share Ferrari facts and lore and to work the 365GTB/4 and his admiration for the car into each conversation. Every quarter or so, Reeg renewed his offer to free up a Daytona's worth of floor space in Doc's garage. This is the way it's done—a gentlemen's game of request and decline.

In business and rare cars alike, it's good to have an inside man. Doc's son Greg knew Reeg and was certain that this long-time neighbor was earnest in his appreciation for Doc and his rare Italian classics. As Greg spoke of the Ferraris in the Frost household, he began calling the coupe "Stan's car."

Reeg maintained a respectful and persistent interest in the closed-body Daytona. Doc wasn't using it anymore. The characteristic cammy snarl that all Ferraristas know had not been heard on the breeze in a long time. St. Donatus's children had been left to dream of football and baseball.

After two years of focused effort, son and car-suitor prevailed and Reeg fulfilled his silent, decades-old promise to call one of Doc Frost's Ferraris his own. His third Ferrari, the Daytona, was a car Reeg had learned well for his own betterment and to prove his competence to the good doctor. Ferrari built only about 1,260 of the coupes. Virtually every nonconsumable component on his purchase was the one that came on the car. Original paint, original interior, engine, transmission. Doc had the original tires, now worn, mounted to the original Borrani wire wheels and they came with the car. A second unused set of identical Michelin XWXs Doc bought in 1972 were also included. Doc also had a set of Cromodora wheels mounted with original Michelin XWXs that he would fit for high-speed touring in Europe. The car came with a set of these too.

The coupe had seen little use since the 1980s. Such an undisturbed find is exciting, but environmental and chemical

There's a reason Daytonas cause a commotion, and it isn't because Don Johnson drove one on *Miami Vice*. It's the V-12 engine that does it, sporting six two-barrel carbs. Reeg's required a rebuild not long after he bought the car from Doc Frost, who hadn't been using it much. Fast cars like to be driven, not stored!

The original leather seats are still comfortable. They show their thirty-five years. The Frosts used these cars. Wear left by a family Reeg admired does not constitute damage so much as character marks.

agents take no time-outs. When cars aren't run and their systems warmed up, lubricated, and moved around to stop oxidation, gunk, evaporation, and shrinkage, a long idle car prefers to stay idle. The first thing Reeg had to do was rebuild the brakes. After 250 miles, the engine stuck, so he had to rebuild that. He then went through all the car's systems, cleaning things up to make them run right.

Reeg ran the car for two years with its original paint, which was heavily applied when the car was new and had cracked to the metal with a spider-web look throughout. Rather than let it decay further, he decided to redo it in the correct red. The original black leather interior and carpeting, as special ordered by Doc, he is leaving as is; that wear comes from his hero, Dr. Frost, using the car with his family as Enzo Ferrari (and Sergio Scaglietti) intended. Such marks, including the one made by the bean-bag ashtray Luella Frost always had in the car, are pleasant reminders of the car's unique history.

As much as the original components, Reeg cherishes the documentation and photos Doc compiled. He considered his trips to Italy business ventures for his performance company, so he documented them thoroughly. It's one thing for a buyer to hear that the car was picked up in Italy and another to see a photo of it in a crowd of Ferraris on the factory floor, or with

Many circular gauges arrayed before the driver's eyes emphasize that this is a performance car. The sporting driver wants to know what his machine is doing and that all systems are functioning properly.

This is no concours interior. "Sit down and drive," is the message here. Getting all the different materials in a car interior to look—and stay—the same color is a challenge, even for Enzo's legendary shops. Of course, the gauges, wheel, and shifter are more important to an owner/ driver than what a flash photo does to color impressions.

the Doc and his wife in various European cities. The doctor set down voluminous details of where the car went, on what days, at what speeds, when serviced, where, and at what cost. Such details validate the car's authenticity and originality and also enrich Reeg's understanding of his well-known doctor-neighbor, the man Numero Uno met in person and whose car he drove, and made right, personally, before releasing it from his revered factory.

In 1972, this was a high-fashion door design. Today it is, and looks like, a classic original door panel. No swap-outs here. This is the door Luella opened and closed when she and the Doc unleashed the V-12.

No wonder Reeg's neighbor was well known in town. You'd have to have no car gene, or simply be clueless, to not appreciate this prancing horse lineup. This shot shows off the Doc's '71 spyder, '72 coupe (now Reeg's), and '73 coupe.

The car that Enzo built—and Scaglietti adjusted and Doc picked up and Reeg admired and pursued and bought—still has guts behind its glory. Rebuilt to its original output of 352 horsepower, the thirty-six-year-old super car has no problems keeping up with modern or classic machinery. Reeg has friends in a Porsche 911 club, who invited him to attend an event they held in LaCrosse, Wisconsin. Afterward, the German coupes—and one Italian—headed off to some rural roads. Even pilots of modern 911s enjoyed the sound and the fury of Reeg's venerable Ferrari 365 GTB/4.

He knew they would. Reeg had spent more than half his life dreaming of summer afternoons unleashing that twelve-cylinder howl on a quiet stretch of road when the shadows are long. Times like that are as good as it gets.

In states like Pennsylvania that see snow and salt, twenty years is about the tail end for regularly driven cars. This '89 Mustang GT has been garaged for much of its life and was washed, waxed, and covered before that. Its looks more like a five- or six-year-old car.

CHAPTER 16

The Ramped-Up Garnet Mustang GT

LIKE THE BEACHCOMBER'S METAL DETECTOR, a car buff's eyes scan the landscape for objects of value. Twenty years ago, James Price was car hunting from the modest confines of his 1980 Plymouth Horizon. At Route 202 and Route 1 in Chadds Ford, Pennsylvania, he got a solid hit—buzzer plus the flashing light. His optical car detectors had a Mustang in range, bright red, on a display ramp at Garnet Ford. "Wow," he thought, "that's really cool."

When you're twenty-one, living at home and working your first corporate job, a new set of wheels ranks high on the goals list. Price had his hopes reigned in to a Ford Mustang or a Chevrolet IROC Camaro. There was a Ford color called Cabernet Red he had been fond of, but the brighter shade on the boldly angled pony car covered over it in his mind. The Camaro, likewise, drove out of his thoughts.

Back at the house, he mentioned the car to his father, Jim. To his surprise, his father responded, "Let's go take a look at it." Price figured it would be a joy ride, part of the shopping process, perhaps, or a chance for father and son to spend some time together. He welcomed the offer, though.

At Garnet, the salesman didn't lead them to a similar car, or something more or less expensive; he lowered the ramp and handed over the keys to the bright red 1989 Mustang GT. The car was a five-speed: perfect. The salesman also described a route he wanted the shoppers to follow that would allow some highway miles.

Price had always been a motorhead and engaged in typical teenage stuff, like fishtailing the family's '70 Mercury Marquis

Here's another set of forces that can affect classics in various ways. Except for a minor toy-Jeep incident, the Price kids have had a positive impact. Lately, they've taken such an interest in the car that selling it is no longer an option.

and a prior hand-me-down slant-six Chrysler LeBaron in parking lots when there was fresh snow. The Mustang was a different sort of animal. The ride was stiffer and more responsive than his prior family cars, and it had more oomph. A soft rain had fallen in Chadds Ford before they got to the dealership and the road was still wet when they departed in the brand new car.

Entering a highway on-ramp for a straight-shot power test, Price put his foot in it—and suddenly the two generations were looking the wrong way. "When the rear-end started coming around it was pretty frightening," he says. Somehow, his father took it in stride. Maybe, inside, he even laughed—it's not so easy to shake up a World War II veteran with a little civilian-car test drive.

When they returned to the dealership, his father didn't head for their own car. He lingered to see what his son had in mind. Even after Price and the salesman got into specifics, Jim made no move to go. Son and salesman negotiated until the dealership man hit a number he stood on: $14,800. Jim said he wanted a word with his son. Price expected to hear that it was time to leave; instead, this particular evening became one of those moments when a father yields more trust to a maturing son.

Despite aluminum's imperviousness to rust, wheels can corrode and discolor when exposed to various chemicals that find their way onto roads. These still look good, though Price says the fronts are hard to keep clean of brake dust.

"If you want this thing," Jim said, "I'll help you with some down money." With that on the table, the salesman sweetened the deal by another three hundred bucks. The car Price had gaped at a few hours before just became his 5.0-liter Mustang GT . . . with factory headers, alloy wheels, PS/PB/PL, air conditioning, AM/FM cassette, and a respectable 225 horsepower with the factory headers.

"We never considered insuring it," Price laughs. "There's something about a twenty-one-year-old kid in a high-powered Mustang. . . . I remember quotes as high as $12,000 a year!" Finally one insurer quoted him a couple grand, and the rate would drop every six months if he didn't have an accident. "I've never had an accident," he says, "and that agent is still my agent."

The on-ramp tail-kick convinced Price that his new car was something he couldn't man-handle, at least not with the skills he'd used on a slant-six LeBaron in a snowy parking lot. Ah, but youth can get the best of us. On a rainy afternoon later in the year, he dropped his girlfriend off at the sprawling King of Prussia mall and got on the highway headed for home. It was rush hour and he began weaving through traffic trying, pointlessly, to find a channel moving much faster—or, as he

All the hoses and clamps are original on this engine and still in good, serviceable condition. Two items not fitted at the Ford factory are the battery, naturally, and the shiny alternator peaking out below the top radiator hose.

put it, "playing pole position." Veering into a fresh gap, he spied something in the road and jerked the wheel to the left to avoid it. At the same instant he realized it was just cardboard, but he had committed.

The back end broke loose and came up beside him. He made a quick correction. Instead of stepping smoothly into place, the rear snapped the other way and kept on going. He spun into the soft median, which grabbed the back tires; the front end slid to a stop pointing straight out at traffic. His brain took a moment to right itself before the stream of cars passing inches from his bumper took shape.

He hopped out. His beloved Mustang was axle-deep in mud and wasn't gonna budge under its own power.

Via maneuvers he can't remember or even picture, he darted across the busy highway on foot to reach the right side of Route 202. (Back then, at least in Pennsylvania, the right lane was the slow lane—a practice the nation seems to be abandoning—and the proper spot to try to bum a ride.) Another driver took pity and gave him a lift home.

The carpets show a little wear after twenty years, as do the pedal pads. This was a daily driver for many years and has more than 116,000 miles. The seats and dash are still in good shape.

Fortunately for Price, a high-school classmate owned a towing service and after traffic had died down, he backed up to the 'Stang, hooked up a cable, and pulled it clear of the mud. Afterward, it rode terribly, shuddering and bouncing down the road. Price thought he'd wrecked the suspension and dreaded a major repair bill—and an explanation to his father. Back at his house, however, he could see that the wheels were packed with mud. He wobbled out to the local carwash and blasted them with a pressure washer. A good cleaning was all it took.

Price grew up by some neighborhood motorheads, lending a wrench or a spare pair of hands when opportunity arose. He remembers helping a teenage neighbor up the street put new carpets in his Triumph while another kid tried to jump over it, hurdler style. Crosswise was a success; the planned lengthwise jump, possibly while the car was driving to shorten required air time, was wisely abandoned. Safety glass is reasonably strong but not meant to stop a six-foot, four-inch basketball player who's pretty sure he can clear it—"if I time it right."

The passenger floor has seen less use and therefore has less wear. The seat side shows slight wear next to the mechanism for tilting the seat back forward. The glove box door still fits square and snug.

Inspired by such tinkering, Price tackled repairs on his own family's cars, from oil changes to a complete rebuild of their 1970 Mercury Marquis Brougham automatic transmission. The latter tested his self-taught skills. When he separated the case and tiny springs leapt out like crickets, some doubt joined them skittering across the concrete floor. It all went together though, renewed with a rebuild kit, and bolstered his confidence for home repairs.

Car folks often fall into one of two camps: the wrench turners and the polishers. A few enjoy both making a mess and cleaning one up, and that's Price. Throughout the car's early years, in addition to doing all the routine maintenance, he was a tireless washer and polisher. After much trial and error, he arrived at the perfect combination to clean and protect. A friend of his mother's sold Amway products door-to-door, and he swears by their car wash soap. "It has a slippery additive," he says. "It makes the sponge glide. With this nonmetallic finish,

Cars that get used also collect beauty marks. Price's daughter bumped the car here with her own transportation, a Purple Power Wheels toy Jeep. No one was injured in the collision, though Dad found out.

every speck of dust you drag across leaves a spider-web-looking scratch." He follows that with Mother's (car care products) three-step program of cleaner, glaze, and swirl remover, and carnauba wax. It leaves a clear gleaming finish, but it isn't quick. "It's like washing a car three times," Price notes. "Who's got time for that, other than a twenty-one-year-old single guy?" As a married father of three today, he keeps waiting for the same chunk of time, and it never comes.

To feed kids, buy clothes, and pay for a house, toys, and all of life's other expenses, he works the corporate scene by day and has a landscaping business nights and weekends. The Mustang fell to occasional use and then to none at all. For the last four years, it has sat silent in his southeastern Pennsylvania garage.

Thanks to conscientious maintenance and cleaning, the car is incredibly original. Price likes it just as it came off the ramp at Garnet Ford and he has never been motivated to hop up the engine, swap out the wheels, scrap the factory stereo, or even cut speaker holes into the doors or deck lid. The plugs have been changed. ". . . [M]ight have put in plug wires," he adds. "If I did, they're original Motorcraft." The tires have been replaced, and need to be again, and naturally it's had a few batteries. It's got the original hoses and clamps, though, and while the air cleaner is not what Ford fitted, it's the same K&N system he installed when the car was almost new, in the Ford housing. "You can buy those expensive lamp-shade-looking things," he adds, "but I

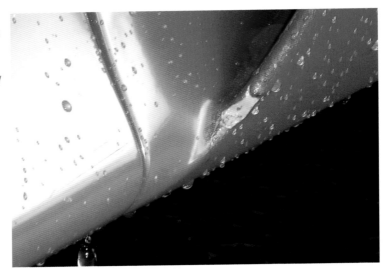

Price can't get mad at his daughter for a little mark that will buff out. He christened the bodywork himself early in the Mustang's life when he ran over an exhaust system on an exit ramp. The setup was complete from downpipe to tailpipe, and there was no way to avoid it.

never did." This setup cleans up with a garden hose and a re-oiler. He's had the same system in place almost twenty years.

Its transition to storage and his family obligations had Price wondering about his Mustang's future. "If you had asked me [its fate] a year ago, I would have said, 'probably clean it up and sell it.' But my son Alex is ten now and he's really gotten interested in cars. He probably knows more about them than any other ten year old. Every time he has to speak in school, he talks about cars. He provides so many details, his teacher once asked, 'Are you making this stuff up?' Alex is fanatical about me keeping the Mustang. I'd feel like I was doing something wrong if I sold it."

The home mechanic with two jobs—landscaping turns to snowplowing over the winter—doesn't have time for all of his own vehicle maintenance anymore. Luckily another high-school classmate opened his own car repair service. Pennsylvania requires vehicle inspections, and he discovered his classmate's shop way back in the LeBaron days. "He really knew his stuff," Price says, and he's used him for jobs too time-consuming for himself ever since.

That connection, like the Mustang itself, seemed meant to be: The first time Price brought the car there, his friend stepped back and took a lingering look at it. "You know," he said, "I

Original paint, washed and waxed often and with great care during the owner's bachelor days, still looks bright. The vague suggestion in this photo that the front end is darker is a trick of the light, probably from the camera's flash.

The clean reflections here show how straight the body is and that the paint holds its shine. Pennsylvania requires no front license plate, but there is a vehicle-inspection program that provides window stickers telling when any car was last street legal.

test drove a Mustang just like this. They had it up on a ramp at Garnet Ford down by 202 and Route 1." Price walked to the back of the car, in view of the dealer sticker, now outlined by a thin border of carnauba wax. "That's this car," he said. "I bought if off that ramp."

If son Alex has his way, he'll be telling the same story years from now—in perfect detail, and this all-original Mustang will look just as good then as it does today.

Index